Mental Subnormality in the Community

Mental Subnormality

DEDICATION

To Leonard W. Mayo, whose lifelong interest in the problems of handicap and specific concern with mental subnormality, both as Director of the Association for the Aid of Crippled Children and as Chairman of the President's Commission on Mental Retardation in the U.S.A., did much to make the present study a reality.

A CLINICAL AND EPIDEMIOLOGIC STUDY
in the Community

HERBERT G. BIRCH
STEPHEN A. RICHARDSON
SIR DUGALD BAIRD
GORDON HOROBIN
RAYMOND ILLSLEY

The Williams & Wilkins Co. / Baltimore 1970

Made in the United States of America

Library of Congress Catalog Card Number 72–116633

SBN 683–00742–4

Composed and printed at the
Waverly Press, Inc.
Mt. Royal and Guilford Aves.
Baltimore, Md. 21202, U.S.A.

Preface

The epidemiologic and clinical study of all mentally subnormal children of a defined age range in a city of 200,000 people cannot be carried out by the zeal or good intentions of the investigators alone. It requires the cooperation of a large number of clinical, research, educational, administrative, clerical, technical, and secretarial resources and the recognition that deficiencies, resistances, or constrictions of full support in any of these can make a mockery of the best laid plans.

In our study we have had the benefit of unstinting support from many agencies and individuals. No formal statement of acknowledgment can even in small measure discharge our indebtedness. It can only serve to record our profound appreciation for the help that we have received from a host of colleagues and friends who, through their efforts, concerns, and interest, helped to make this study a reality. We hope that they will share with us what is of worth in this book. We ourselves must accept, unshared, the responsibilities for its shortcomings.

We wish to thank the educational authority of Aberdeen, and particularly Mr. James R. Clark, Director of Education in Aberdeen, and Mr. Ian McKinnon, Headmaster, Aberdeen Special Schools, as well as Mr. Hugh McRae, Schools Psychologist, and Mr. George G. Yule, Chief Schools Welfare Officer. They, together with the teachers at the schools, wholeheartedly aided in our study of the children and by their kindness and interest in the investigation continuously contributed to the morale and enthusiasm of the scientific team.

We wish to thank, too, the health authority, Dr. Ian A. G. MacQueen, Medical Officer of Health and Director of Social Welfare of Aberdeen, and his associates, Miss Margaret Nairn, Superintendent Health Visitor and Coordinating Nursing Officer, Dr. William J. W. Rae, Junior Deputy Medical Officer of Health, Miss Mary Sangster, Specialist Health Visitor, Beechwood School After-care, Miss Dorothy D. Strachan, Mental After-care Officer, and Dr. Dorothy Younie, formerly Senior

v

Assistant Medical Officer, for countless items of information and for the fullest availability of medical information.

We also wish to thank the obstetricians and pediatricians who, over the years, established the basis for an epidemiologic analysis of obstetric antecedents and whose years of record keeping made it possible to define clinical complications. In particular, we express our gratitude to Mr. Ian MacGillivray, Professor of Obstetrics and Gynaecology, Dr. John Craig, Emeritus Professor of Child Health, Dr. Ian M. Lowit, Consultant Child Psychiatrist, Dr. W. Malcolm Millar, Professor of Mental Health, and Dr. Ross G. Mitchell, Professor of Child Health.

Our thanks also go to the members of the Obstetric Medicine Research Unit and its successor, the Medical Social Research Unit, and particularly to Mr. David Oldman, Sociologist, Mr. W. Z. Billewicz, Statistician, Mr. William R. Bytheway, Statistician, Mrs. Angela M. Finlayson, Sociologist, Mrs. Ruth M. Holliday, Statistician, Miss Margaret E. Milne, Administrative Assistant, and Dr. Angus M. Thompson, now Director of the Reproduction and Growth Research Unit.

We thank, too, Dr. James G. Henderson, Director of the Special Homes and Schools for Mentally Subnormal Children, and Miss Violet Sullivan, Matron, Woodlands Home.

The study that we have made would have been impossible without the work of a mixed team of medical and psychologic specialists who evaluated the mentally subnormal children. We give particular thanks to Mrs. Joy Baldwin, Dr. Ira Belmont, Dr. Morton and Mrs. Juliet Bortner, Dr. Margaret Hertzig, Dr. Michael Rutter, and Dr. Lawrence T. Taft, whose book this is as much as it is ours.

We express deep appreciation to a number of other persons who, through their devoted attention to problems of data analysis, administration, and composition, made continuous contributions to this volume. We can take only this quite inadequate form of acknowledging the help of Mrs. Ida Hafner, Miss Katherine Entenberg, and Miss Elvia Cohn.

To Mrs. Dothlyn Dennis, who carefully handled and sorted mountains of data, and to Mrs. Laura Vajda, who struggled often and sometimes with success to improve our prose, we offer special thanks.

Studies of whole populations of children are not only difficult but also expensive. This study could not have been carried out without the continuing support that the collaborating teams of investigators received from the Medical Research Council, the National Institutes of Health, National Institute of Child Health and Human Development (Grant HD00719), and most particularly the Association for the Aid of Crippled Children, New York. To these agencies we give thanks for both personal and material support.

Contents

Part One

MENTAL SUBNORMALITY IN THE
COMMUNITY

1

The Motives and Background for the Study

This book reports a clinical and epidemiologic study of the prevalence, distribution, and antecedents of mental subnormality in 8- to 10-year-old children living in a medium-sized city. Such a study was carried out because great concern is expressed today about the size of the problem of mental subnormality. In the U.S.A. this concern is reflected at least partially in the substance of the report of the President's Panel on Mental Retardation (1962), which estimated that in that country mental subnormality incapacitated 10 times as many individuals as did diabetes and 600 times as many as were affected by poliomyelitis. The report indicated further that, if current trends in the U.S.A. continued, it could be anticipated that at least 126,000 infants born each year in that country would at some point in life be classified as mentally subnormal. Against this background, the study reported in this book was undertaken with the view that an attempt to establish some epidemiologic and clinical facts about mental subnormality might more fully elucidate its social distribution and its etiology.

We have had to recognize that it is difficult enough to cope with a social and health problem of this magnitude when the disorder considered is a single etiologic entity or even a homogeneous syndrome of dysfunction; the task becomes even more complex when this is not the case and when one appreciates that mental subnormality "is a constellation of syndromes. It is not a disease, although it may be the result of a disease. It is more accurate to describe it as a condition that affects from 2 to 3 percent of the total population. Its principal characteristic is retarded intellectual development and inability to adapt to demands of society" (Stevens, 1964). Given this common feature of outcome,

3

expressed in a heterogeneity of patterns of symptom and etiology, it is our belief that effective intervention—whether for the rational planning of services or for the development of useful methods of prevention— depends upon sound knowledge of the prevalence and differential distribution of intellectual dysfunction and of its subvariants in the community. We further believe that, if such distributions can be related to antecedent health experience and to the social and family background, a sound basis may be established for developing useful hypotheses about causes. In short, it was our hope that a joint clinical and epidemiologic analysis of mental subnormality in a defined age range of children within the total population of a city could "provide quantitative information to (1) estimate the size, nature, and location of the community's problems; (2) identify the component parts of the problem; (3) locate populations at special risk of being affected; and (4) identify opportunities for preventive work and need for treatment and special services" (Gruenberg, 1964).

For several reasons, the city of Aberdeen was felt to be an appropriate setting in which to pursue such inquiries. In the first place, its administrative atmosphere was congenial for the investigation and contained cooperative school and health authorities with an interest in mental subnormality and its clinical characteristics, well-developed special school and health services for mentally subnormal children, and a broadly-applied, uniform system of psychometric testing for the ascertainment of intellectual level in children of school age. Second, for more than a decade, a joint obstetric, statistical, and sociologic team (Medical Research Council, Obstetric Medicine Research Unit) had, in a standardized manner, collected and recorded information of good quality on the social, familial, and health characteristics of almost all mothers and on the course and complications of almost all pregnancies and deliveries occurring in the community. Third, the community was relatively stable, with a high proportion of the children born in the city still in residence 10 years after the time of their birth. Given these conditions and the positive interest of the administrative authorities in a more detailed evaluation of mentally subnormal children, it was possible not only to identify but also clinically to assess the current functioning of all children who, in a given age group, had been identified as mentally subnormal, to relate these findings to their medical and social antecedents, and to compare these findings with those obtaining for the remainder of the children of the same age in the general population.

We have, therefore, in this community conducted an inquiry:

1. To determine the prevalence of mental subnormality in a defined age range;

2. To describe the mentally subnormal children identified in terms of the degree of severity of their mental defect and the presence or absence of associated clinically demonstrable signs of central nervous system damage and psychiatric disorder;

3. To examine the degree to which mental subnormality and its association or lack of association with clinically demonstrable neurologic and psychiatric disorder was distributed in various social class segments of the community;

4. To examine the association of obstetric and perinatal antecedents with mental subnormality and its associated neurologic features;

5. To examine the interrelations of social, familial, and health conditions in mental subnormality and its subvariants; and

6. To identify interactions between the biologic and social factors associated with mental subnormality.

We shall now briefly consider the several aspects of the investigation.

Estimating the Prevalance of Mental Subnormality

The first step in seeking to understand a health phenomenon is the study of its prevalence and distribution—a task not easy in the area of mental subnormality. In any community, estimates of the prevalence of this dysfunction may be affected by the manner in which the disability is defined, by the social conditions of life, by the levels of demand for cognitive and adaptive functioning that society makes of its members, by the amount and quality of the services that are available, by the age range considered, and by the criteria of dysfunction that are utilized for identification of cases. Consequently, findings on prevalence vary and, despite general agreement that mental subnormality constitutes a major category of disability in children, determination of a "true" prevalence is probably both misleading and impossible. However, it is always possible and of value to make the "best" estimate of prevalence at a given point in time if the various factors which influence prevalence level are taken into account. A brief review of some of these factors is therefore appropriate at this point.

The Definition of Mental Subnormality. Clearly, before one can investigate either the prevalence or the antecedents of any set of syndromes, the dysfunction to be studied must be defined. For no disorder does this truism have greater cogency than for mental subnormality. The particular need for clarity in definition derives directly from the fact that mental subnormality is, as Wechsler (1944) has put it, "unlike typhoid fever or general paresis ... not a disease. A mental defective is not a person who suffers from a specific disease process, but one who by reason of intellectual arrest or impairment is unable to cope with his environment to the extent that he needs special care, education, and (sometimes) institutionalization." Further, the phenomenon of arrested or incomplete development of mind is not a uniform clinical entity but a common end product which does not stem from any single and readily identifiable pattern of cause.

Systematic concern with defining mental subnormality had its origin in legal matters and, in the first place, involved the need to make a distinction between those individuals who were permanently and presumably congenitally arrested in the development of mind and those who were merely transiently incapable of making complex social adaptations and of assuming responsibility for their acts. Such a distinction was first made in England in the time of Edward I, when the law differentiated between those who were mentally subnormal, and therefore presumably permanently incapable of ordering their affairs, and those who were transiently unable to do so for reasons of acute or chronic mental illness. The legal distinction was carried forward into medicine by Thomas Willis, the discoverer of the path of intracranial circulation, who suggested that it was essential for the clinician to distinguish the psychotic from the defective and argued that it was useful to devise a separate clinical category for the "foolish" as contrasted with the "stupid" (*cf.* Cranefield, 1961).

Interest in identifying those in the population who were mentally subnormal as well as efforts to define familial and environmental causes of the dysfunction have continued over several centuries and, indeed, persist until today. However, during the latter half of the 19th century, the transition from an agricultural to an industrial society accompanied by a shift from rural to urban living served both to increase social concern with the problem of mental subnormality and to promote its more frequent identification. The technologic complexity of industry and the changed nature of work together with the demands for literacy that accompanied these changes were reflected in the development of expanded programs of free and compulsory education—the academic character of which resulted in an increase in the number of children who, during the school years, were identified as mentally subnormal. As the facilities for compulsory public education expanded, the absolute number of children who were identified as being unable to profit from such education steadily increased. However, as Tredgold (1952) has indicated, "At the close of the century the only defectives generally recognized were those of low grade, idiots and imbeciles, and the number of these was comparatively small."

With the expansion of public education, school failure came to be viewed as often deriving from primary mental incapacity. It was, therefore, not surprising to find that in several different settings consideration was given to the development of sensitive and efficient methods for identifying potentially educationally inadequate or mentally subnormal children early in life and, in particular, well in advance of school failure. It was believed that, if such methods could be developed, the social and personal cost of identifying the mentally subnormal child through his manifest incompetence in school could be avoided and more effective and earlier planning for his special training could be undertaken. The most notable of such efforts to identify children who were mentally subnormal were those of Binet and Simon (1911), in France. These students of the problem, with training in education, medicine, and comparative psychology, set out to develop a method for the early identification of children with poor potential for successful school achievement. The result of their work, a mental "scale" later made into a test of intelligence, is too well known in its original form, in its many modifications, and in the variety of devices for estimating mental functioning which it has inspired, to require any detailed discussion (Stoddard, 1947). From the point of view of the history of the identification of mental subnormality, what is of importance is that the test and its successors provided an additional objective, functional measure of mental subnormality.

Because of its ease in administration and the apparent accuracy of its numerical score, the psychometric test has sometimes been applied without due regard for its dependence upon cultural and experiential uniformity in the population studied (Anastasi, 1963) and has been unjustly criticized as a result. However, the psychometric tests together with the criteria of social incompetence and school failure have expanded the range of identified mental subnormality to include, in addition to the more severely impaired, a class of "feebleminded, who are three times more numerous" (Tredgold, 1952).

In the present study, prevalence has been estimated through the use of social, educational, and psychometric criteria. The children identified range in their mental subnormality from severe to mild degrees of incompetence and span the total range of currently identifiable levels of intellectual impairment.

Age. The overall prevalence of identified mental subnormality varies with the age of the group considered. Since, under conditions of modern life, the most carefully observed responses to systematic demands for intellectual functioning, for a very wide segment of the population, occur within the school setting, and these demands increase in complexity over the school years, it is not surprising that the proportion of individuals who come to be identified as mentally subnormal increases with school age. Educational failure itself is so important a factor in bringing mental subnormality to notice that, only half in jest, one public health authority has called universal free compulsory education the single largest "cause" of mental subnormality (Stevenson, 1956). After the school years many persons classified at school as being mentally subnormal are reabsorbed into the community and their poor intellectual functioning becomes less relevant and less noticeable in a non-educational setting (*cf.* Gruenberg, 1964).

The increasing ease of identification with age, up to adolescence, and consequent changes in age-specific prevalence rates are neatly illustrated by the data on prevalence presented by Lewis in his analysis of the Wood Committee Report on Mental Subnormality in England and Wales (1929). In this survey the estimated prevalence of mentally subnormal individuals in the population ranged from 1.2 per 1000 in the children under 4 years of age to 25.6 per 1000 in the age group of 10 to 14 years. After school-leaving age (14 years), the number of individuals in the population socially identified as being mentally subnormal steadily decreased until, by the age range of 50 to 59 years, the noted prevalence had dropped to 4.9 per 1000—a drop not accounted for by differential death rates.

For the reasons already mentioned, data from different countries on the absolute prevalence of mental subnormality are non-comparable. However, relative prevalence at different ages may usefully be considered. In a recent survey, Gruenberg (1964) has made this analysis and has shown that, in spite of the difference in the reported prevalence for such different communities as Formosa, England, Scandinavia, and Onondaga County in New York State, the curves for the age-specific rates of noted prevalence are remarkably similar in shape, showing a steady rise to peak levels during the school years and a steady decline thereafter.

In the present study the children range in age from 8 to 10 years and the prevalence figures therefore reflect the sum of all cases identified up to this age less those identified earlier who either have died or have left the community. Clearly, by this age not all children who will eventually be identified as mentally subnormal have come to notice and it is anticipated that the prevalence rate will increase until the children leave school at 15 years of age, the permissible age of school-leaving.

Availability of Facilities for Diagnosis and Management. Noted prevalence levels for mental subnormality, as for any disorder, are highly correlated with the facilities available for diagnosis and treatment. In Aberdeen, both the procedures for diagnosis and the facilities for special education and care (to be described in Chapter 2) are exceptionally good and make it unlikely that many cases have been missed because of insufficient diagnostic, remedial treatment, or educational services. Moreover, the psychometric screening of virtually the whole school population at 7 years of age in this community has made it possible to identify practically all psychometrically subnormal children, including those who have not been administratively designated as mentally subnormal.

In Aberdeen, therefore, the prevalence of mental subnormality reflects the demands of a modern industrial society with free, universal, and compulsory public education and the psychometric screening of virtually all children at 7 years of age. We can therefore be reasonably confident that the population of subnormal children under review reflects the actual frequency of the disorder in the community and provides a sound basis for analyzing the distribution of both the characteristics of current functioning and certain features of the social and biologic antecedents in such children.

Subtypes of Mental Subnormality

It is probable that in many cases mental subnormality is the result of the interaction of a variety of disorders. In our attempt to identify these more precisely, all cases were individually and independently examined by a psychologist, a neurologist, and a psychiatrist and were classified with respect to severity of intellectual impairment and to presence or absence of associated central nervous system damage and psychiatric abnormality. These facts were related to the health history of the child and the social background. In the past the degree of severity of intellectual impairment has been the criterion most frequently applied for internal differentiation within the broad category of mental subnormality. Using this criterion, Lewis (1929) and O'Connor and Tizard (1956) found that the ratios of estimated prevalence of severe to moderate to mild subnormality were to one another as 1 to 4 to 15.

In traditional functional terms, therefore, they estimated that 5 percent of the mentally subnormal functioned as "idiots," 20 percent as "imbeciles," and 75 percent as "feebleminded." Translated into intelligence test scores, these findings mean that 25 percent of the noted mentally subnormal have IQs below 50 and 75 percent have IQs between 50 and 75.

Clinically diagnosed central nervous system damage and behavioral aberration have been intermittently considered in some selected clinical populations of mentally subnormal children (Masland *et al*, 1958; Benton, 1964) but have not been used systematically as criteria for differentiating among clinical subtypes in community studies. Obtaining such data for a total population sample provides us with new information on (1) the extent to which clinically manifested neurologic or psychiatric signs are associated with mental subnormality, (2) the frequency with which each is manifested when intellectual impairment is of different degree, (3) their relation to one another, and (4) the association of these clinically defined subvariants of mental subnormality with both current and antecedent biologic and social factors. Clearly, the search for causes of mental subnormality is facilitated by such information.

The Search for Cause

For the great majority of cases of mental subnormality, we have little knowledge of cause. There are probably three broad categories of antecedent causes—genetic and familial factors, biologic insults to which the child is exposed before, during, and after his birth, and a substandard social and physical environment, which, while not causing direct physical damage, may influence the course of his intellectual growth and development.

Since the 19th century, there have been major swings in opinion as to the relative importance of genetic and environmental factors in the causation of mental subnormality. Until recently, evidence for a genetic etiology rested on studies of the genealogies of persons with mental subnormality and sibship analyses of such cases (*e.g.*, Penrose, 1963; Tredgold, 1952). Data such as those of Goddard (1912), deriving from a retrospective analysis of the Kallikak family, were used as evidence to support a genetic explanation of mental subnormality. However, in this and in other studies, methodologic weaknesses made firm conclusions difficult. These included the failure to recognize the poor quality and incompleteness of the anecdotal data upon which the findings were based and the inability to separate the effects of living conditions, social environment, and habits of the families on mental handicap from those of genetic origin. In more recent times the development of biochemical methods and human cytogenetics as well as improved methods for studying population genetics have made it possible to examine the genetics of mental defect in a more systematic fashion, to confirm certain genetic speculations and reject others, and to define the existence of specific genetic defects in some cases of mental subnormality.

Despite the fundamental biologic importance of the genetic studies. recent reviews of mental subnormality (Masland *et al*, 1958; Penrose, 1963; Knobloch & Pasamanick, 1962) have concluded that only a very small proportion of the total cases of mental subnormality could be accounted for by specific biochemical-genetic etiologies. Knobloch and Pasamanick (1962) have sought to estimate the relative magnitude of the contribution made by these specific genetic factors and by other etiologic factors in the production of mental subnormality, and they suggest that even the most frequently occurring genetic anomaly, the one resulting in Down's Syndrome, "is only one-tenth as frequent as mental subnormality due to prenatal and perinatal abnormalities." They have argued on these grounds that the epidemiologic study of the events surrounding pregnancy and birth is urgently needed. The present study reflects agreement with this identification of need but goes a step further by focusing not only on the reproductive process but also upon the broader social environment for growth and development as well.

Obstetricians and pediatricians have long maintained that there is a relationship between severe mental subnormality in children and maternal complications during pregnancy and/or prolonged or complicated deliveries. There have been numerous studies, reviewed by MacMahon and Sowa (1961), Knobloch and Pasamanick (1962), and Montague (1962), implicating a variety of pregnancy, delivery, and postnatal complications in the production of mental subnormality. However, it must be pointed out that the presence of complications of pregnancy or labor does not prove that they "cause" mental subnormality; they might simply coexist. It is known, for example, that the prevalence of mental subnormality increases as the social environment of children worsens. It is probable that the incidence and severity of obstetric factors vary in the same way. It is, therefore, necessary to control for general environmental circumstances which are reflected by social class position. In short, an analysis of complications and of their relation to the production of mental subnormality demands an epidemiologic study in which social class is clearly defined.

However, a concern with the implications of social environment for the production of mental subnormality is far broader than the need to control for social variables in considering the possible contributions to cause made by obstetric and perinatal complications. Social environment, disadvantages, and deprivation have in themselves been implicated as etiologies for the general inhibition of mental development and the production of mental subnormality (Masland *et al*, 1958; Hunt, 1961; Stein & Susser, 1960). Consequently, social factors and features of the family environment must, in their own right, be considered as contributors to cause.

Considerations in Epidemiologic Study

In a general sense epidemiology may be considered as a method which defines the conditions in which a disorder arises and persists by analyzing its distribution in the populations in which it is found. It involves, too, the analysis and interpretation of the patterns of these distributions of the disorder in relation to possible causal factors. However, as Dawber *et al* (1963) have put it, "epidemiologic study suggests guilt by association.... It is unusual for an epidemiologic study to provide positive proof of the 'cause' of a disease.... More often epidemiologic studies point the way to fruitful areas for definitive research into causal factors.... (Moreover) ... such studies can point the way to prevention long before the cause or cure for the disease is discovered" (pp. 540 to 541).

By determining associations, fruitful areas for more detailed research may be identified and possible paths for prevention may be defined. If, in addition, the obtained association is strong and may plausibly or clinically be linked to a pathogenetic sequence, the probability of "cause" is heightened though never proven.

The tasks of epidemiologic analysis in mental subnormality are complicated by the fact that the consideration of antecedents to the dysfunction requires a relatively long-term longitudinal follow-up study. The time gap between the occurrence of most of the known or implicated causal factors and the point in time at which mental subnormality itself can be definitely diagnosed is often very long. Most of the biologic factors thought to cause mental subnormality (except for instances of postnatal insult) occur between the child's conception and the first weeks of life, but the diagnosis of mental subnormality, unless it is of severe degree, cannot usually be reliably established until much later in life. For most cases of mental subnormality of mild degree, a gap of 7 or 8 years exists and creates formidable problems for the conduct of longitudinal research.

The availability of data of good quality over such a prolonged time span has not been present for whole populations. Investigators have, therefore, been forced to use samples of unknown bias because relevant data were at least partially available for such samples or to use poor retrospective data. Moreover, potential sources of bias deriving from such phenomena as selective migration and death have been difficult to assess.

One solution for these difficulties is the selection of a sample for study which is either a defined group of mentally subnormal children having clear reference to a total population or a birth cohort that can be meaningfully described. Neither is easy to do since, if the investigator selects as his group for study the children in an institution giving residential care, the sample tends to be a selected segment of the more severely subnormal, is unlikely to be representative of all severe cases, and is subject to both known and unknown selection biases. Other problems of bias are present when the investigator starts out by selecting all or a sample of births from a given obstetric hospital. He has no assurance that the records for such births are representative of any defined geographic area or population. For example, university teaching hospitals, in which records may be good, often tend to be referral centers which selectively serve higher risk cases and have no systematic information on the persons in the population who do not come to the particular hospital. It is apparent that, although such biased samples may usefully be studied for some purposes, they cannot be used for defining conditions of risk for mental subnormality in the community as a whole.

These considerations led us to decide that a community-wide study was necessary to provide a fuller and more valid view of the interaction of biologic and social factors associated with mental subnormality and to provide information on the best estimated prevalence and social distribution of the dysfunction and on the potential etiologic factors with which the disorder is associated. In order to cope with the problems described above, we chose a community which had the following characteristics:

1. It was large and relatively isolated with very little in- or outmigration and was a city in which selective migration could be assessed;

2. Obstetric and neonatal records of high quality had been kept in

a uniform manner for the total population of births, and obstetric services of good quality were available to all women;

3. Medical services were available irrespective of ability to pay;

4. An effective and uniform set of screening procedures was in force throughout the community for identifying mentally subnormal children;

5. Research and administrative personnel within the community had an active interest in carrying out a community-wide study of mental subnormality;

6. Uniform diagnostic examinations of all mentally subnormal children could be performed to confirm the diagnosis of mental subnormality, to assess its degree of severity, and to determine its association with central nervous system damage and psychiatric abnormality.

In analyzing the associations between mental subnormality and antecedent events, we have followed a step-wise procedure which hopefully has resulted in a clearer explication of these associations and a sharper definition of risk conditions. In these analyses we have continuously borne in mind the fact that the wide array of variables suggested as possible "causes" of mental subnormality are not independent of one another. Pregnancy complication is associated with prematurity, which in its turn has a strong association with jaundice, respiratory distress, twinning, etc. For these reasons an analysis of the association of obstetric complications with mental subnormality demands a detailed clinical obstetric consideration of a wide variety of factors, both in isolation and in combination with one another. In the present study we have sought to deal with these difficulties by

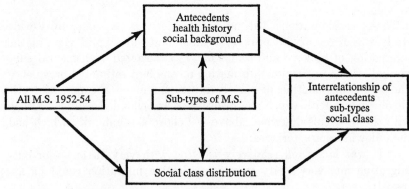

Figure 1. A schematic view of the study. M.S., mental subnormality. Left side of figure indicates children born 1952 to 1954.

combining epidemiologic and clinical findings in the analysis of mental subnormality and its antecedents.

Our procedure in the analysis of the data is schematically presented in Figure 1.

As may be seen from the figure, we start our analysis by identifying all surviving mentally subnormal children in three pooled annual cohorts of births who still resided in the community at the time of study. The distribution of these children is next considered. The subvariants of mental subnormality are defined and related to social class. Mental subnormality as a whole, its clinical subvariants, and their distribution by social class are then analyzed with respect to obstetric, social, and familial antecedents.

2

The Setting and Design of the Study

Aberdeen, Scotland, a community which best met the criteria that we had defined, was the city selected for study. It is a large urban center with a relatively stable population and a good administrative structure for the identification of mentally subnormal children. All pregnancies and deliveries have been followed by defined procedures for almost 20 years and uniform antenatal and perinatal records of high quality are available for the total population of births. Since 1951, social information including data on migration, social class, marital status, housing area, and family background has been collected systematically for the total population. From the neonatal period through the school years, health records and uniform objective educational records are maintained for all city children. The availability of these data coupled with both the strong interest in research on problems of mental subnormality and the markedly cooperative attitude toward investigation in all relevant agencies and administrative departments dictated the choice of community.

Because the findings of the study rest heavily upon both the nature of the community and the nature of available records, it is essential to describe these in some detail.

The Setting and the Children*

Aberdeen, the third largest city in Scotland, is situated on the northeast coast and in 1961 had a population of approximately 187,000 people. No large suburbs exist outside of the city limits and there are no large adjacent towns, the nearest large town, Dundee, being 70 miles

---

*For this description, we have drawn upon *Aberdeen's Health and Welfare Services: An Introduction for Visitors from Overseas,* prepared by the Medical Officer of Health, Dr. I. A. G. MacQueen.

distant. The city is a seaport with a large fishing fleet. It is also an industrial, commercial, and educational center and has an agricultural hinterland about 40 miles broad extending to the west before the land rises steeply to form the Grampian Mountains. The industries include shipbuilding, manufacture of machinery, textiles, paper, and wool, and granite quarrying. During the summer it is a holiday resort. It is the main commercial and cultural center for the northeast region of Scotland and is the home of the University of Aberdeen and of colleges of technology and education. It is also the center of the Regional Hospital Board, which, under the National Health Service, is responsible for specialist medical services for the region, and is a center for agricultural and fisheries research.

As a result of Aberdeen's birth rate of approximately 3000 children each year, some 30,000 children are enrolled in the schools. Since the Director of Education has responsibility for the general overview of both municipal and private schools, it is possible to be concerned with all school children through a single administrative authority.

In addition to maintaining complete records on every child's academic progress, Aberdeen's Department of Education administers standard achievement tests at ages 7, 9, and 11. These tests are also administered in some of the private schools and the results were made available to the research team for this study. We therefore have test results at age 7 for 98 percent of the city children. Because the Roman Catholic and other private schools do not have special facilities for handicapped children, all children needing special educational facilities are provided with such services by the city schools.

Identifying children who require special education for reasons of mental subnormality is an ongoing feature of the educational system. Unless a child is very severely retarded, he enters school at 5 in a regular class placement and remains in regular classes until, at the age of 7, he takes the standard achievement test mentioned above. Any child who scores below 75 on this test is referred for individual psychometric evaluation by a psychologist and, when individual testing indicates that the child has an IQ below 75, the test findings together with recommendations from the psychologist are sent to the School Medical Officer. This officer evaluates the child's whole situation by relating the psychologic findings to the child's current health, past history, and all other examination results. As part of the general evaluative procedure, the School Medical Officer may ask the head of the child's school to submit information on his school achievement and any other information, such as behavior or patterns of play, that he feels may be pertinent to the evaluation. At this time, the headmaster may make a recommendation as to the child's proper school placement.

The evaluation and general recommendation together with the psychologic test information and other pertinent data are recorded on a standard form for statutory reasons. The completed form, the supporting material from the psychologist, the contributions of the headmaster, and the recommendation of the School Medical Officer are then sent to the Director of Education, who reviews the entire case. He discusses the situation with the child's parents and makes his own recommendation to the Education Committee.

If the Education Committee approves the recommendation, the Director of Education is free to implement it. The Director of Education is required to communicate with the parents in writing, stating his recommendation and its basis and pointing out to them their right to appeal against the decision—first to the educational authorities in Aberdeen and then, if they wish, to the Secretary of State for Scotland. When an appeal is made to the Secretary, his representatives review the entire dossier and make an independent judgment. Their decision is then sent in writing to the parents, with a copy to the educational authorities.

In addition to the statutory procedure described above, there is a system of voluntary referral. If they wish, parents may send their child to a special school for mentally subnormal children on a trial basis in order to determine whether such an arrangement is in his best interests. If the parents are not satisfied with their child's progress in the special school, they can insist that he be returned to a regular school. If, on the other hand, they feel that placement in the special school is appropriate, voluntary referral can be made statutory.

Special placement may be made at once for children whose mental subnormality is evident on school entrance.

Special provisions have been made for the educational needs of mentally subnormal children. For educable mentally subnormal children, a large, well-equipped building with accommodation for approximately 500 children has been provided. Because it was built specifically for physically and mentally handicapped children, this school incorporates in its design the special facilities and equipment required for their education. Another school has been provided to meet the needs of trainable subnormal children, and the Regional Hospital Board maintains a residential institution for the most severely retarded children.

The system described functions for all schools in Aberdeen regardless of their auspices. On very rare occasions, children who have multiple handicaps or severe psychiatric illness may be sent to a residential facility outside of the city. However, since cases are known to the school authorities and are identifiable, all children who are mentally subnormal as defined by the administrative procedures described above are known to the educational authorities.

The criteria used in the Aberdeen screening and evaluation of children for mental subnormality reflect the view that no single measure is adequate and that identification must be based upon an overall evaluation of the child—that is, his intellectual, physical, and social functioning as well as his school performance. Clearly, the classification of a child as mentally subnormal may be influenced by the nature of the special educational facilities that are available. If the special physical and personnel resources are overtaxed or inferior in quality, teachers, physicians, and parents may be reluctant to identify and categorize a child as mentally subnormal. Such a classification would be pointless if no special facilities existed for the child or even harmful if it placed the child in overcrowded or inadequate settings. This bias in classification is unlikely to occur in Aberdeen because of the generous provision of physical facilities for the mentally subnormal and because of the quality of the teaching staff.

The general attitude in Aberdeen toward the teaching of handicapped children is that it calls for a high level of skill and experience on the part of teachers. Only those who are experienced and successful in teaching normal school children and who express a strong interest in handicapped children are selected for special training. The teacher remains on salary and all training costs are borne by the educational authorities. Those teachers who successfully complete the special training earn a higher salary than do teachers in the regular schools.

However, even in the most favorable setting for the classification of mental subnormality, a discrepancy may occur between populations of mentally subnormal children identified and classified by multiple criteria and those based on a single measure, such as performance on an intelligence test. On p. 31, we estimate the number of children who might be classified as mentally subnormal on the basis of IQ distribution alone and compare this figure with the actual population identified by the screening process described above.

Maternity and Health Records. After the end of World War II, a number of events took place that made it possible to develop a system of record collection and storage to provide information on the social background, pregnancies, and deliveries of the total population of Aberdeen. Moreover, the establishment of the National Health Service in 1947 resulted in a considerable degree of unification of obstetric care. Many services were transferred to the Maternity Hospital, which shortly came to provide antenatal and maternity services for more than 85 percent of all pregnancies in the city. Maternity care for domiciliary births was provided by the National Health Service. Cooperation of midwives, general practitioners, and obstetricians is good and all records of these non-hospital births are tranferred to the Maternity Hospital on special forms matched to the Maternity Hospital records. Since 1948, all maternity records have been coded and placed on punch cards, thus making them readily available for statistical analysis.

Opportunities for the acquisition, organization, and processing of maternity data for the total population of the city were improved in 1948 by the establishment of a Medical Research Council Research Team, especially devoted to obstetric research. This team, which, from its inception, included an epidemiologist and a statistician, was augmented in 1951 to include a full-time research sociologist. Consequently, since that date, the obstetric records have included sociologic information, much of which is obtained routinely on all cases, and some of which was collected for given samples on an *ad hoc* basis in connection with special studies.

Through its Health Visitors Service, the City Department of Health maintains systematic records of all health visits, which are made to every child in the city several times a year from birth until school age. From these records it is possible to obtain the dates at which children attain the developmental landmarks, evidence of significant illness, and indications of the adequacy of child care. After children enter the school system, the School Medical Officer is responsible for evaluating their health. Health record cards are maintained on every child throughout his school career, and hospital records are also available for children who have been hospitalized.

Design of the Study

Given the available records on the total population of normal and mentally subnormal children, a choice had to be made as to the direction the present inquiry should take. The information available at the start of the study included obstetric data on all Aberdeen births since 1948 and information on the screening and classification of school children for mental subnormality. Either body of data could be used as the basis for defining the study population, the decision depending upon which of two study designs was chosen.

One approach is to start with the population of children who are identified as mentally subnormal and move back in time to determine the antecedent events associated with mental subnormality by comparing this population of children with those in the same birth years who are not mentally subnormal. Alternatively, one can begin with certain complications of pregnancy, delivery, or early childhood which, on the basis of previous research and theory, are believed to contribute to the development of mental subnormality and follow up those children at presumed risk to determine whether mental subnormality occurs more often in association with a given complication than in its absence. The first approach begins with children who are mentally subnormal and leads back in a search for causal factors. The alternative design begins with "factors" believed to contribute to the causes of mental subnormality and traces their consequences forward in time.

Given our research objectives of determining the prevalence of mental subnormality in the community, of learning more about the individual characteristics of children who are mentally subnormal, and of uncovering various biologic and social environmental factors which are associated with mental subnormality, we chose the first direction and started with the population of mentally retarded children as our initial point of reference.

For the most part, the design of the study was influenced by two facts already mentioned in Chapter 1: (1) that the age-specific prevalence of the disorder changes with age, with increasingly large numbers of children being designated as mentally subnormal from infancy to the age of school-leaving, and (2) that the severity of subnormality, as well as the frequency of physical handicaps associated with it, varies inversely with age at identification—the younger identified being more severely retarded in mental development and having a higher frequency of associated disabilities. For these reasons a concern with prevalence and etiology in mental subnormality requires the study of children in defined age groups.

A number of reasons led to the decision to limit the age range of the children selected for the present study to 8 to 10 years inclusive. By so limiting the group, one would be dealing with a narrow age span but with one which would include all children identified as subnormal in the preschool period and through 3 years of schooling as well as through the use of a general screening test administered to all 7-year-old children in the school system. In addition, because of the school-leaving age of 15 years, such a group would be available within the school system for follow-up over the next 5 years.

The age range studied was selected, also, for the reason of excellence of background health and maternity records. Since this study was conducted in 1962, the population selected contained all children in Aberdeen classified as mentally subnormal by the local authorities and born in 1952, 1953, and 1954. The records for these birth years are fully available and, having been pretested and used in final form since 1948, they are of high quality.

We estimate, on the basis of available data (Penrose, 1954; O'Connor & Tizard, 1956; Gruenberg, 1964) on the age-specific prevalence of mental subnormality, that approximately 100 children in the 3 birth years would be identified as mentally subnormal. In fact, the number of children identified was as follows:

Place of Residence (1962)	Number of children identified by place of birth (1952 to 1954)		
	Aberdeen	Elsewhere	All
Aberdeen	97	7	104
Elsewhere	—	4	4
All	97	11	108

The core population of children born in Aberdeen and still resident there 8 to 10 years later amounts to 97, making this group relevant for the analysis of the association between obstetric factors and mental subnormality. However, in dealing with this subject in Chapters 8 and 9, we use a population of 92, which excludes five children whose mental subnormality is clearly attributable to non-obstetric factors (four mongols, one measles encephalitis).

In the study of prevalence we are concerned with all mentally subnormal children resident in Aberdeen, whatever their place of birth. This gives a total of 104 children used in Chapter 3.

The composition of populations used for the analyses in separate chapters is set out below:

Chapter	Population	Exclusions
3–4	104	4 non-residents
6–7	98	4 non-residents, 5 mongols (1 being a non-Aberdeen birth), and 1 postencephalitic
8–9	92	4 non-residents, 6 non-Aberdeen births, 5 mongols, and 1 postencephalitic (as above)

The scheme used in this study for categorizing social class is a modification of the British Registrar General's (1951) scheme based on occupation of the head of the household. In the British system, several occupations roughly comparable in social and economic terms are grouped together as follows to form five social classes.

Social class	Description	Examples
I	Professional	Doctor, lawyer, company director, minister of religion
II	Intermediate	Teacher, trained nurse or midwife, shopkeeper, commercial or industrial manager, highly skilled technician
III	Skilled	Clerk, postman, joiner, fitter, bricklayer, lorry driver, merchant seaman
IV	Partly skilled	Fisherman, agricultural laborer, bus conductor, packer
V	Unskilled	Laborer, railway porter, road sweeper

This classification was not fully appropriate for the present study because it results in groups of unequal size, with 3.3 percent of the population falling into Social Class I and 52.9 percent falling into Social Class III. Thus, in order to obtain groupings of relatively equal size, Social Class III has been subdivided into three groups and the scheme has been revised as follows:

Social class	Description
I–IIIa	Non-manual
IIIb	Journeyman and artisan
IIIc	Other skilled manual
IV	Semiskilled manual
V	Unskilled manual

Possible Selective Effects of Migration. In estimating the prevalence and social distribution of subnormality, the use of a population consisting of both "sedentes" (*i.e.*, born and still resident in the city) and in-migrants raises the issue of the selective effect of migration. Were the children who left Aberdeen between 1952 to 1954, the years of birth, and 1962, the time of study, biased with respect to mental subnormality in general or to any one of its subvariants? To what extent were the out-migrants balanced in absolute numbers or in social and intellectual composition by in-migrants over the same period? This problem may be approached either by examining the data of the present study for evidence of selective effects of migration or by presenting general data gathered from many sources about migration processes among young families in Aberdeen.

The first approach involves a comparison of available data for sedentes, out-migrants, and in-migrants in our study population. Only two relevant items of information are available—the number of children in each group and their father's social class. Before this study was begun (December 1962), 1850 children born in Aberdeen in 1952 to 1954 had left the city. Although they were partially replaced by 929 children born elsewhere, there was obviously a net loss by migration. Out-migration shows a clear social class gradient which rises from 10 percent in Class V to 51 percent in Class I, with social class based on father's occupation at the time of birth of the child (1952 to 1954). In-migration was even more sharply skewed toward the upper social groups, but in this case social class was based on occupation at the time of the study (1962). The net result of migratory move is therefore the unreplaced loss of 921 children (10 percent of the original birth population) drawn disproportionately from the upper social groups.

How is this likely to affect our findings? Migration in Britain is most frequent in upper social groups, whereas the prevalence of mental subnormality is highest in lower social groups (see Chapter 5). An area of net in-migration, because of its higher social composition, is therefore likely to have a relatively low prevalence of mental subnormality. An area of net out-migration, such as Aberdeen, whose out-migrant upper groups are not fully replaced by equivalent in-migrants, has a relatively high prevalence. The differences, however, are small. We obtain a prevalence of 12 per 1000. If the in-migrant population and its mentally subnormal group were doubled so as to fully replace the out-migrants, prevalence would be 12.1 per 1000. Moreover, our prevalence findings are based on all 8- to 10-year-old children living in Aberdeen in December 1962 and, regardless of previous migratory movements, they are a true statement of known prevalence in 8- to 10-year-old children at that point in time.

When we turn from prevalence to the social distribution of mental subnormality, its subvariants, and its obstetric etiology, it becomes apparent that our findings might be distorted if either out- or in-migration were associated with some aspect of subnormality—e.g., if middle class parents left the city rather than have their child attend the special school or if parents who had children with a particular form of handicap were advised to educate them in some other area.

Before the present study began, an inquiry into differential migration had been completed. On the basis of this work (Illsley et al, 1963), it was found that, of the children born in the city, approximately 85 percent would still be in residence after a 5-year period. This figure is a conservative estimate based upon primiparae. One would expect greater residential stability in the total population of childbearing women because the frequency of migration tends to fall with age and increasing family size. This general level of population stability is clearly advantageous for a longitudinal community study. Rates of out-migration in Aberdeen were highest in young people and in the professional and non-manual groups and lowest in older families and among unskilled workers, a finding common to most studies of migration in advanced industrial societies. The association of social class and age with health, physique, and education also means that the out-migrants were relatively well-educated, had high performance in intelligence tests, were above average in stature, and had low rates for those complications, such as perinatal death and low birth weight, which are influenced by poverty, poor nutrition, etc.

The *residual* population used for comparison purposes throughout this study is therefore biased toward the lower social classes, and rates of complications are not fully representative of those pertaining to the original total population of births. Our purpose in these analyses, however, is to compare the characteristics of the residual group of mentally subnormal children with the residual (*i.e.*, non-migrant) population from which they are drawn. Differential migration would therefore affect our conclusions only if the mentally subnormal group migrated out of the city at a higher or lower rate than the remainder.

Because migrants are drawn disproportionately from upper socio-economic groups and because the incidence of identified subnormality is usually highest in the lower socio-economic groups, analyses throughout this volume, whenever possible, have been carried out within class groupings. Again, whenever relevant, comparisons are made between an index child and its siblings, a procedure which obviates the influences of selective bias as a consequence of differential migration.

Although we have social, demographic, and obstetric background information on out-migrants, we do not know the level of intellectual functioning of the children in this group. We therefore do not know whether, within given social class, age, and pregnancy groupings or in certain segments of the population, mentally subnormal children migrate more or less frequently than do the remainder of the population. Out-migration is high at young ages and in primiparae and the highest rates of migration occur within the year immediately following delivery. Thus, most parents migrate before the intellectual status of their child is known.

In a community known to be relatively rich in services for the mentally subnormal, the presence of a mentally subnormal child might act to dissuade the parents from migrating. On the other hand, parents who resist the identification, classification, and educational treatment of their child as mentally subnormal might be stimulated to migrate to an area with less adequate services, where their child is more likely to be educated in the ordinary schools and is less likely to be singled out for special attention. Such behavior would be most likely in middle class parents with a mildly retarded child.

Differential Evaluation of the Mentally Subnormal Children. Each of the 104 mentally subnormal children was individually evaluated for intellectual level, clinical neurologic findings, and psychiatric status. These examinations† were carried out by a highly qualified team of clinical examiners. With the close cooperation of the school and health authorities, members of the research team, who were experienced clinicians, gave each child in the selected mentally subnormal population a psychologic,‡ pediatric-neurologic, and psychiatric examination. Each member of the professional team made his evaluation without having any access to either the Aberdeen authorities' education and health records or the results of any of the tests conducted by other members of the research team. They did, however, know that the children had been classified by the local authorities as mentally subnormal and whether the child had been placed in the residential institution for severely retarded children or in a school for trainable or educable children.

Background Factors Associated with Mental Subnormality. Records available in Aberdeen were used to identify the background factors associated with mental subnormality. The details and definitions of the various background factors are presented in later chapters in association with their analysis. Here, only a summary indicative of the range of inquiry is presented.

Broadly considered, the available records provided information on two types of background feature—biologic and social. Biologic information included data on the physical characteristics of the child's mother, the nature of the pregnancy, labor, and delivery of which he was the product, his condition as a newborn infant, and his health history. These data result in the following list of variables in terms of which the mentally subnormal children may be considered:

Mother	*Child*
Height	Gestational age and birth weight
Age at time of pregnancy	Neonatal status
Parity	Childhood accidents and illnesses
Complications of pregnancy and delivery	
Duration of labor	
Multiple births	
Previous pregnancy outcomes	

† Each one is described in the following chapters.
‡ Where a child was severely mentally subnormal, standard tests were clearly inappropriate and clinical assessment of functioning was made.

Social information was available from two sources—the records, which provided information on the mother's family background, education, and premarital occupation as well as on her and her husband's social class, and a detailed questionnaire, which was administered to the families of all of the mentally subnormal children and to a 1 in 5 random sample of the families of children in the comparison population. The questionnaire provided information on current social circumstances, housing, family size, and economic status. Together, the two sources contributed the following variables for consideration:

From records	*From questionnaires*
Mother's family social class	Father's social class at time of study
Mother's education	Number of persons per room in the child's home
Mother's height	
Mother's premarital occupation	Number of siblings
Husband's social class	Ordinal position of mentally subnormal child
	Unemployment of father

Analysis of the Data. The three bodies of data—(1) differential clinical consideration of the mentally subnormal children, (2) biologic background information, and (3) social information—made it possible to consider factors associated with mental subnormality from two points of view. One, which we shall call an external analysis, is to compare the background histories of the population of mentally subnormal children with all or a sample of children who are not subnormal and who are of the same ages to determine, for example, whether subnormal children have lower birth weights than do children who are not subnormal. The other, an internal analysis, is to make comparisons, within the population of mentally subnormal children, of those with different clinical varieties of subnormality to see, for example, whether severely subnormal children have lower birth weights than do mildly subnormal children. In most instances both analytic approaches are used. On occasion, however, one may be for various reasons either meaningless or inappropriate and, therefore, omitted.

3

The Prevalence of Mental Subnormality

In the present chapter we seek to make a "complete" estimate of the prevalence of mentally subnormal children aged 8 through 10 years, resident in Aberdeen, and born in 1952 to 1954. There are at least two reasons for doing so. The first, and perhaps more important from the standpoint of the scientific value of the study, is that knowledge of prevalence is essential as a basis for defining the degree to which findings in Aberdeen are likely to be representative of other communities. The second, more important in a practical sense, is that accurate information on prevalence is necessary as a basis for defining needs and planning for the establishment of remedial services.

It is a truism that an epidemiologic inquiry in a given community is, in fact, a case study of that community. The results that are obtained, the inferences that are drawn, and the conclusions that may be derived are bound at every point to the specific time and place in which the study has been conducted. In the strictest sense, therefore, the conclusions which may be drawn from the study of a given community are applicable only to itself, and strict determination of the cross-comparability of any set of findings is, in the final analysis, dependent upon the replication of the study in a number of settings.

In the absence of such replication, the extent to which the findings of any study may be generalized and transferred depends upon (1) the degree to which the community studied is appropriately representative of a class of communities in its social and ethnic composition, its circumstances for life, and its conditions for work, and (2) the degree to which the communities are equivalent in opportunties for ascertainment of mental subnormality.

We may summarize these considerations by noting that prevalence depends upon (1) the criteria of mental subnormality, (2) the completeness of identification, (3) the incidence of causally relevant familial, genetic, or biologic factors, and (4) the cultural level of the population in relation to the criteria used.

Differences in prevalence between communities may, therefore, be attributable to differences in one or all of these factors. Similarities in prevalence can arise through different weightings of these factors. We can, therefore, use prevalence data to make comparisons between communities in respect to one of the above factors only when the others are known to be in agreement. Consequently, it is essential, as a first step, to identify features of Aberdeen which may influence the prevalence of mental subnormality in the community.

Characteristics of Aberdeen Which May Influence Prevalence

As an urban center of approximately 200,000 which performs administrative, service, industrial, and mercantile functions both for its own inhabitants and for a surrounding rural area, Aberdeen is not markedly different from many other large urban communities. It may, however, differ from such communities in two important respects.

First, its population is unusually stable and tends to be ethnically homogeneous, the great majority being of Scottish descent. Consequently, it does not contain any significant minority groups, which may be noted frequently in more cosmopolitan urban centers. Since a host of factors may place these groups at a notable disadvantage both in school situations and on psychometric tests, these minorities may contribute a disproportionate number of individuals who are designated as mentally subnormal.

Secondly, the practice of sterilization as a means of controlling family size tends to be more widespread in Aberdeen than in many other urban centers (*cf.* Baird, 1965). Conversely, excellent facilities in the community for the ascertainment of mental subnormality may tend to increase the prevalence rate unduly.

Prevalence of Mental Subnormality in 8- to 10-Year-Olds

Our first consideration of the prevalence of mental subnormality is based on children in the relevant age groups who, at the time of the study, were classified by the local authorities as mentally subnormal and were placed by them in special custodial training or educational facilities. Of the total 8274 children in the age range who are resident in Aberdeen, 104 have been identified as subnormal by the local authorities in accordance with conjoined considerations of social competence, school performance, medical findings, and psychometric level (a rate of

12.6 per 1000). They were reexamined for the present study with the resulting confirmation of the designation that had been made by the local authorities.

This estimate of prevalence must be considered as minimal. Numerous workers in the field of mental subnormality (*cf.* Tizard, 1964; O'Connor & Tizard, 1958) have noted that "in almost all communities there will be a number of children who, on psychometric grounds, should be designated as mentally subnormal who remain in ordinary schools." Reasons for the failure to identify such children as mentally subnormal are numerous and include the judgment that their best interests are served and their best learning progress is made if they remain in the ordinary schools, sometimes repeating grades and, in certain circumstances, receiving remedial instruction. If one is to make a fuller estimate of the prevalence of mental subnormality in a community, these administratively undesignated children must be included.

In Aberdeen it was possible to identify these children because of the almost universal administration of a psychometric test to children when they are 7 years old. This test, the Moray House Picture Test of Intelligence, was taken by more than 95 percent of all children in the birth years considered, and we have used a score of less than 75 on this test as psychometric evidence of mental subnormality. By doing so, we have identified an additional 123 children who, when they were 7 years old, had test scores of less than 75 but who had not been adminstratively designated as being mentally subnormal. Thus, in addition to the group that had been administratively defined as mentally subnormal, there were 14.9 children per 1000 in the city who were performing at a psychometrically subnormal level. If these children are added to those who had been administratively designated, the total prevalence of mentally subnormal children per 1000 in the 8- to 10-year age range is 27.4 (see Table 1).

Clearly, features of the social distribution of administratively ascertained mental subnormality could be influenced by the degree to which

TABLE 1.

Prevalence of mental subnormality and borderline subnormality for children aged 8 to 10, resident in the city of Aberdeen, and born in 1952 to 1954

Means of Classification as Mentally Subnormal	No. of Children	Prevalence per 1000
Administrative	104	12.6
Psychometric (children in ordinary schools)	123	14.9
Best estimate of overall prevalence	227	27.4

TABLE 2.
Ascertained and unascertained cases of mild mental subnormality
(IQ ≥ 60) by social class

Social Class	No. of Ascertained Cases	No. of Unascertained Cases
I–IIIa	0	8
IIIb	3	24
IIIc	10	30
IV	13	22
V	26	34
X*	—	5
Total	52	123

* Illegitimate cases.

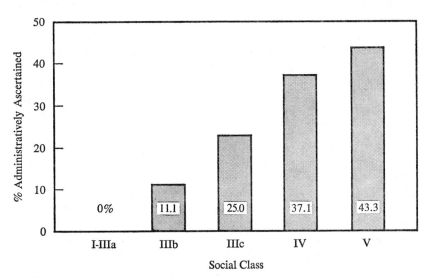

Figure 1. The relation of social class to the frequency with which mild mental subnormality is administratively ascertained.

social bias affected ascertainment. This bias can be estimated by contrasting the number of ascertained and unascertained cases of mental subnormality with IQs above 60 in each social class. When this is done (Table 2), the data suggest that a bias exists and that lower class children with mild levels of psychometric subnormality are more readily ascertained administratively and placed in special school settings for the mentally subnormal.

In Figure 1 are presented the proportions of mildly subnormal children in each social class who were administratively ascertained as being subnormal. It is clear from these data that, if IQ alone is used as the criterion of mental subnormality, there is a social class gradient, with administrative ascertainment of such cases being most complete in the lowest and most incomplete in the highest social class.

Such bias in ascertainment is restricted to cases with the mildest degrees of intellectual impairment and does not affect conclusions with respect to prevalence in cases showing more severe depression of IQ.

Overall Prevalence of Mental Subnormality in Aberdeen and Other Communities

Studies of prevalence that have been conducted in social settings most comparable with Aberdeen are those carried out by Goodman and Tizard (1962) in London and Middlesex and by Stein and Susser (1960) and Susser and Kushlick (1961) in Salford (an industrial suburb of Manchester). Both of these sites were chosen for study because, as Goodman and Tizard have noted, "they are regions in which services are already fairly adequate" and where levels of ascertainment are consequently expected to be high. In both cases, the prevalence figures presented have been based on "ascertained cases, that is, cases which have actually been brought to the notice of the local health authority."

As may be noted in Table 3, the prevalence figures for London, Middlesex, and Salford are slightly higher than those noted in the earlier study of prevalence of mental subnormality carried out in the late 1920s for England and Wales by Lewis (1929). In this study, several ascertainment procedures, including records, teachers' assessments, and individual psychometric and clinical evaluations, were used for identification of cases. It is of interest to note that, although Lewis' study was conducted more than 30 years before the current one in Aberdeen, the methods used in identifying cases were quite similar.

In the United States, prevalence rates of mental subnormality in children are available for the city of Baltimore as a result of a study by Lemkau, Tietze, and Cooper (1943), and, in non-English-speaking regions, a prevalence study for eight Dutch towns has been reported by the World Health Organization (1954). In these studies, prevalence figures were derived from a search of records from medical, social, and educational agencies. Despite the differences in methods of ascertainment and in the times at which the studies were conducted, the estimates of prevalence obtained in Aberdeen are similar to the figures derived from comparable studies in urban centers (Table 3). The Aberdeen "complete" estimate of 27.4 per 1000 is somewhat higher

TABLE 3.

Summary of overall prevalence rates (per 1000) of mental subnormality in children reported in various studies*

Study Location	Age of Children	Prevalence per 1000
London	5–9	36.0
	10–14	45.3
Middlesex County	5–9	30.1
	10–14	36.1
Salford†	5–9	19.8
	10–14	28.4
England and Wales, overall best estimate of urban areas	7–14	20.9
Baltimore, Md., U.S.A.	5–9	11.8
	10–14	43.6
Netherlands (8 cities)	All ages	26.0
Aberdeen, Scotland	8–10	27.4

* The Aberdeen figures are based on administrative ascertainment and clinical reassessment, whereas the others are most heavily based on administrative ascertainment only.

† The Salford (1961) figures are quoted as 19.8 and 28.4, respectively, in Kushlick: Assessing the size of the problem of subnormality. In Meade, J. E., and Parkes, A. S., Eds., Genetic and Environmental Factors in Human Ability. Eugenics Society Symposium, London: Oliver & Boyd, 1966.

than the prevalence figures obtained by Lewis (1929) in his survey of England and Wales, is almost identical with the Dutch figures, and falls within the prevalence ranges reported for Salford (1961) and Baltimore. It is somewhat lower than the estimates for London and Middlesex (1964), a difference which may derive in whole or in part from differences in ethnic homogeneity of the populations studied and the degree to which the study area is representative of the whole urban area in which it is situated. On the whole, these comparisons of overall prevalence support the view that, insofar as prevalence of mental subnormality is concerned, the results of the Aberdeen study may have general applicability.

It may well be argued that differences in prevalence across communities derive at least in part from differences in the completeness with which communities identify as mentally subnormal those children who are at the mild or borderline levels of severity of intellectual impairment. Whether such children are noted depends, among other factors, upon the demands made by the specific school system, upon the availability of diagnostic and treatment facilities within the community, and upon the degree to which the educational system is able and willing to retain slow learners in the regular school grades. As a consequence, it may be suggested that a sounder basis for comparing the prevalence of mental subnormality in Aberdeen with that found in other communities may be achieved by restricting our consideration of prevalence to those mentally subnormal children who are more severely impaired —namely, those with IQs of less than 50.

In general, children with such levels of intellectual impairment are the segment of the mentally subnormal population most fully ascertained in any community that has reasonably adequate school and health

TABLE 4.

Comparison of the prevalence rates of IQ under 50 in age groups where all subjects are likely to be known

Study Location and Year	Age of Children	Total Rate per 1000 of IQ < 50
England and Wales (Lewis, 1929) 1925–1927 urban	7–14	3.71†
Middlesex (Goodman & Tizard, 1962) 1960	7–14	3.45
1960	10–14	3.61
Salford (Susser & Kushlick, 1961) 1961	15–19	3.64
Wessex (Kushlick, 1964) 1964 county boroughs	15–19	3.54
1964 counties	15–19	3.84
Baltimore, Md., U.S.A. (Lemkau *et al*, 1943) 1936	10–14	3.3
Aberdeen, Scotland 1962	8–10	3.7

* This table is a summary prepared by Kushlick (1964). We have added the Aberdeen figure.

† Rate is 3.76 in Lewis' table.

services, and these children tend to be indentified before school entrance. Moreover, since the prevalence rate for severe mental subnormality does not show the kind of regular increase with age so common for mental subnormality in general, it is possible to compare such rates for severely subnormal children of different age ranges.

Prevalence of Mentally Subnormal Children with IQs of Less than 50 in Aberdeen and Other Communities

When consideration is restricted to children with IQs of less than 50, a prevalence rate of 3.7 per 1000 is obtained for 8- to 10-year-old children in Aberdeen. As may be seen from the data presented in Table 4, this rate agrees very closely with the rates reported in other studies. It is almost identical with the rates reported for England and Wales, Middlesex, Salford, and Wessex and the county boroughs (1964) and is only slightly higher than the rate reported for Baltimore.

These similarities in prevalence rate across communities of mentally subnormal children whose IQs are less than 50 increase our confidence that the findings which result from the study of mental subnormality and its antecedents in Aberdeen may be generalized and transferred to other urban communities of similar social composition.

Both the general characteristics of Aberdeen as an urban community and the distribution of mental subnormality within it suggest that Aberdeen is not an atypical community but is one in which the analysis of mental subnormality and its subtypes has general relevance. For a fuller understanding of the distribution of the disorder in the community, prevalences have to be related to the social position of the families from which the children derive. Such an analysis, however, will be more meaningful after we have presented a detailed description of the clinical characteristics of the mentally subnormal children in the city. This will make it possible to consider prevalence in relation to the findings obtained on neurologic, psychologic, and psychiatric examinations of the children. It is to these clinical evaluations that we turn in the next chapter.

4

Clinical Subvariants of Mental Subnormality

For the effective planning of services and for identifying opportunities for prevention, we must know more specifically the clinical patterns found in children included under the very general rubric of mental subnormality. To this end we have examined and subdivided our sample of mentally subnormal children with respect to three aspects of function widely used in clinical evaluation: (1) the severity of intellectual impairment, (2) the presence or absence of clinical evidence of central nervous system damage, and (3) the presence or absence of clinical signs of psychiatric or behavioral abnormality. These evaluations have made it possible (1) to determine the distributions of intellectual level, clinical neurologic status, and psychiatric abnormality in a total population sample of mentally subnormal children, (2) to examine the association of these aspects of current functioning with one another, and (3) to identify patterns of clinical dysfunction in each of the children. In this chapter the clinical findings on the children and the procedures from which they are derived are described.

Several comprehensive reviews (Maher, 1963; Garfield, 1963; Malamud, 1964; Beier, 1964; MacMahon & Sowa, 1961; Masland et al, 1958) that have appeared in the literature recently make it clear that, of the three clinical features mentioned, only one, severity of intellectual impairment, has been systematically studied in representative populations. When neurologic and psychiatric attributes have been studied in cases of mental subnormality, the children either were resident in institutions or were series of clinic cases of unknown representativeness and undetermined bias. However, since institutions tend selectively to admit the more severely impaired children and have a disproportionate

36

number of referrals of mentally subnormal persons who have associated psychiatric abnormality (Saenger, 1960), bias has almost certainly been weighted toward excessive severity of intellectual handicap and high frequency of associated neurologic and behavioral abnormality. Since the samples studied have been unrepresentative of mentally subnormal children in any defined age range in a community, we have no data at present on prevalence or incidence of the various clinical subtypes which would have general applicability.

In addition to the problems of sampling, interpretation of earlier findings has been made difficult by possibilities for distortion or bias present in the conditions under which the primary clinical judgment was made. When descriptions of clinical status have included neurologic assessment and psychiatric evaluation as well as a determination of intellectual level, little or no effort has been made to ensure independence in the evaluation of each of the functional measures. As a consequence, the degree to which psychiatric judgment may or may not have been affected by knowledge of neurologic and psychometric findings, or neurologic evaluation by knowledge of behavioral assessments, is unknown.

In the present study we have sought to avoid difficulties in both sampling and potential for contamination at evaluation. The mentally subnormal children studied included all those within a defined age range in a total population, and the findings are referable to the community as a whole and to the entire range of administratively defined mental subnormality found in it, rather than to any delimited segment of the disorder. Except for the fact that the examiners knew the children to be subnormal and were acquainted with the type of care they were receiving, the evaluations of intellectual level, neurologic organization, and psychiatric status were conducted independently of each other, with no examiner aware of the findings obtained or the judgments made by his colleagues. As a result, with the exception noted, each assessment was independent and uncontaminated by knowledge of other concurrent clinical findings and evaluations.

Evaluation of Intellectual Level

Severity of intellectual impairment may be estimated both by the child's school or institutional placement and by psychometric evaluation. In the community that we are studying, the most severely impaired children were either home-bound or in a center which provided total care. Less severely impaired children were classified as "trainable" and attended a special facility established for their training and

TABLE 1.

Distribution of mentally subnormal children in school and institutions and at home

Placement	No. of Children	Percent
Special education............................	84	80.8
Training center.............................	8	7.7
Institution for total care....................	8	7.7
Home-bound................................	4	3.8
Total..	104	100

habilitation. The mentally subnormal children whose intellectual functioning was least severely affected in the main were defined as "educable" and were assigned to a special school. Such placements were based upon the screening, evaluation, and administrative procedures that have been described in Chapter 2.

As may be seen from Table 1, the great majority of the mentally subnormal children were judged to be educable. Of the remainder, equal numbers were in functional habilitation training or in a setting which provided total care. Four children, all intellectually impaired to a severe degree, were cared for at home principally as a result of parental preference.

A more detailed basis for estimating the levels of intellectual functioning in this group of mentally subnormal children is provided by the data from individual psychometric testing carried out as part of the clinical evaluation. The assessments of intellectual level were made by means of the Wechsler Intelligence Scale for Children (WISC), adapted for use with British children. The test item alterations used were those recommended for British children by the Committee of Professional Psychologists of the British Psychological Society. These alterations were minor and involved substituting British for American money in the Arithmetic subtest and specific changes in demands for information and in other verbal items to take into account differences in national background. Since the WISC did not have a sufficiently low "floor" for some of the younger children, the equations developed for the downward extrapolation of IQ by Ogdon (1960) for Full Scale IQ and by Silverstein (1963) for Verbal and Performance IQ were used to assign IQs below those given in the test manual (1949). Such extrapolations were necessary for seven children on Full Scale IQ, for two on Verbal IQ, and for three on Performance IQ.

All WISC examinations were conducted by two experienced examiners, each of whom examined one-half of the children. The examiners checked each other's test protocols and scorings to ensure accuracy and uniformity.

Individual intelligence tests were given to 84 of the 88 mentally subnormal children who were the least severely impaired and who were in special school placement. Illness interfered with testing in two cases and lack of cooperation resulted in incomplete examinations in two others. The children in the training center, in the total-care institution, and at home were not given individual intelligence tests. The levels of mental competence of these children, as well as of the four for whom testing had been impossible or incomplete, were estimated on the basis of direct behavioral observation, history of competence, findings on prior examinations, and current level of functioning in the placement center or at home. These estimates were made to a three-point scale with the highest rating being an IQ of 60 or more, the middle an IQ between 50 and 59, and the lowest an IQ of less than 50.

Findings on Psychometric Evaluation. The distribution of IQ level by sex is presented in Table 2. The findings on IQ presented in this table are, in general, in agreement with the levels of intellectual impairment already noted in terms of placement in custodial and educational settings. If, as is customary, an IQ of less than 50 is taken as a presumptive index of ineducability, 29 percent of the mentally subnormal children were psychometrically classifiable as ineducable and 71 percent could be placed in the educable subnormal category. This classification, of course, is somewhat discrepant with actual placements (Table 1), which included a larger number of children in special educational placement than would have been warranted by a strict application of IQ level alone. Such a discrepancy should not be unexpected since IQ is only one of several criteria used to make a school assignment, with aspects of the child's temperament, motivation, and conduct also contributing in important ways to decisions concerning educational placement. Moreover, in the case of many children with IQ be-

TABLE 2.

Distribution of IQ by sex in mentally subnormal children (aged 8 to 10 years) in Aberdeen

Sex	No. of Children at IQ Level				
	<50	50–59	60–69	≥70	Total
Male..................	17	10	11	19	57
Female...............	14	11	13	9	47
Total.................	31	21	24	28	104

low 50, the school authorities pursued a "benefit of doubt" policy and made an initial assignment to the special school rather than to a training center.

Twelve percent of the children who were socially and administratively classified as mentally subnormal had individual IQs slightly above 75 on individual psychologic testing. That this number of children is functioning at a given moment at a test IQ level slightly above the arbitrary upper limit of IQ required for the administrative designation of mental subnormality is not surprising, since IQ is not a firmly fixed value and is subject to change with age and special training (Haggard, 1954; Hunt, 1961), as well as with interest, motivation, and attitude. Moreover, it is only one of several criteria used for the overall assessment of the functional intellectual integrity of the child.

Since the numbers of boys and of girls in the city who were 8 to 10 years of age were almost equal (49 and 51 percent, respectively), it can be seen from Table 2 that mental subnormality was slightly more prevalent in boys than in girls. The ratio of boys to girls who were subnormal was 56 to 44 percent for the group as a whole. This difference by sex derived largely from significant differences in numbers of mentally subnormal boys and girls in the IQ range 70 and above, with little or no difference in frequency by sex shown in the children whose mental subnormality was of a more severe degree (Figure 1). It will be of interest to explore sex differences at a later point in relation to possible differences by sex in biologic or social antecedents of mental subnormality.

In all subsequent analyses we will use the IQ level of the child as determined by the research staff, rather than his social placement, as the indicator of the degree of his intellectual impairment. This practice is made with full recognition that the identification of a child as mentally subnormal is almost always dependent upon a complex of social, educational, and psychometric indices. However, psychometric level is the only one of these which is likely to be equivalent in different community settings and is therefore of greatest general value for purposes of cross-community comparisons. It is, therefore, of some value to view the psychometric findings in somewhat greater detail.

Since the WISC estimation of intellectual level is based upon two scales—Verbal and Performance—which can be considered independently of each other, one can view the levels of functioning of the children on each of these scales separately. As may be seen in Tables 3 and 4, no significant differences between distributions of Verbal and Performance IQs existed within the group of children tested. However, this lack of overall group difference is in part the result of the existence of two subgroups of children in whom significant differences between Verbal and Performance IQs obtain. These subgroups may be identified if a difference of 10 points or more between Verbal and Performance IQs is used as a cutoff value. When this criterion is used (Table 5), it is found that 18 children have Performance IQs which are 10 points or more higher than their Verbal ones, and 13 children have an equivalent level of difference favoring Verbal IQ. When the sex of the children having a difference of 10 IQ points or more between levels on performance and verbal tasks is considered, a clear trend may be

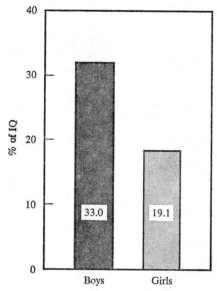

Figure 1. Sex and IQ 70 and above in mentally subnormal children.

TABLE 3.

Distribution of Verbal IQ by sex

Sex	No. of Children at IQ Level				
	< 50	50–59	60–69	≧ 70	Total
Male.....................	3	7	13	21	44
Female.................	3	4	20	9	36
Total...................	6	11	33	30	80

TABLE 4.

Distribution of Performance IQ by sex

Sex	No. of Children at IQ Level				
	<50	50–59	60–69	$\geqq 70$	Total
Male...................	3	4	14	23	44
Female.................	5	7	12	12	36
Total..................	8	11	26	35	80

noted, with the mentally subnormal girls tending to achieve higher scores on verbal tasks and the boys, higher scores on performance tasks. This pattern is not found in normal children.

It is, of course, tempting to consider the patterning of intellectual performances in greater detail. However, such a procedure would divert us from our main purpose, namely, the division of the mentally subnormal children with respect to the degree of severity of their intellectual impairment. More detailed consideration of the patterning of intellectual functioning in these children has been reported elsewhere (Belmont *et al,* 1967; Birch *et al,* 1967).

Clinical Evaluation of Central Nervous System Status

For many years investigators have studied the association of central nervous system damage with mental subnormality as one way in which to define an etiology for the disorder. It has been argued quite properly (Benda & Farrell, 1955; Masland *et al,* 1958; Malamud, 1964) that the finding of pathologic changes in brain or of clinical signs of central nervous system damage increases the likelihood that the observed mental subnormality derives from organic damage to the brain. Clearly, such a conclusion is inferential but has the virtue of parsimony. Maher (p. 241, 1963) has put the issue well in stating that:

Of all the etiological hypotheses offered to account for the clinical cases of mental retardation, perhaps the most common and crucial is that the patient is suffering from organic damage, usually to the central nervous system. Organic damage is generally regarded as an alternative explanation to either environmental deprivation or genetically determined retardation. The practicing clinician is continually faced with the problem of differential diagnosis which this distinction implies. He may be required to decide, on the basis of tests, whether the behavior of the patient is to be attributed to subcultural factors or to organic factors. If the former possibility is eliminated on the basis of test inferences, he may be required to decide whether or not the organic anomaly is to be attributed to genetic determinants or to variables which operated to injure the organic integrity of the patient after conception. If

TABLE 5.

Verbal and Performance IQ discrepancy in mentally subnormal children by sex*

Sex	No. of Children with Performance IQ $\geqq$ Verbal IQ + 10	No. of Children with Verbal IQ $\geqq$ Performance IQ + 10
Male....................................	13	4
Female..................................	5	9
Total...................................	18	13

* $\chi^2 = 3.697$; p $<$ 0.10.

the latter appears to be the case, he may attempt to judge whether or not the injury took place *in utero* or whether it is to be attributed to mechanical assault during or after delivery.

To these considerations one must, of course, add the possibility of post-natal insult (James, 1961).

The identification of central nervous system damage in mentally subnormal children, although almost universally recognized as important, has not been carried out in a systematic way. One set of difficulties in interpreting available data derives from the tendency to study samples of children who are drawn from clinical or institutional settings and has already been considered. However, another type of bias, which has not yet been considered, derives from the nature of clinical and educational practices (*cf.* Birch, 1964). In many settings, facilities for pediatric neurologic evaluation are limited, and only selected children are referred for special study. Such children tend to be those who fit the behavioral stereotype of brain damage (Strauss & Lehtinen, 1950) and represent highly selected samples. A judgment that brain damage is absent in those children not referred is frequently made by default rather than by diagnosis. As a consequence, meaningful generalization from available records is either difficult or impossible.

A further difficulty in interpreting earlier reports stems from the clinical circumstances in which neurologic evaluations have been made. Such evaluations are usually made under conditions in which the neurologist is aware and apprised of the results of psychologic testing, certain aspects of which have been widely assumed to be indicators of brain damage (*cf.* Benton, 1964). Since the neurologist frequently knows the behavioral diagnosis, his evaluations are often colored by the presumptive diagnosis that has already been made on behavioral grounds. Thus, the data are of dubious value as independent identifiers of children having neurologic signs indicative of central nervous system damage.

In the present study we have sought to avoid the difficulties inherent in earlier investigations by the manner in which we have defined our sample and by subjecting the children to a standardized clinical neurologic assessment in full independence of other evaluations. The examination (a schedule for which is presented in Appendix 3) was comprehensive and recorded the following attributes: mental status; orientation; degree of cooperation; speech and language; intactness of cranial nerves; sensory organization; reflexes; directed and voluntary movement; muscle strength and tone; motor coordination; extinction to double simultaneous tactile stimulation; and physical stigmata relevant to neurologic defects.

One hundred and one of the 104 children received such evaluations. Three were not evaluated for reasons of illness. One, a child with orthopedic handicap, was in a full-body cast, and two had acute but persistent illnesses which interfered with reliable neurologic assessment.

All of the neurologic examinations were divided between two examiners who exercised care in standardizing the examination procedures and in ensuring the uniform recording of findings. Decisions on the clinical neurologic status of the children were made from the entire set of examination protocols independently by each of the examiners. Agreement in diagnostic assignment was at a high level, with full agreement in 97 cases and partial agreement, made full after conference, in the remaining four.

A patient was judged to be neurologically abnormal if (1) one localizing ("hard") sign or more of central nervous system abnormality was present, or (2) two non-localizing ("soft") signs or more (Paine & Oppé, 1966) of central nervous system abnormality were found. "Hard" signs included such standard localizing findings of central nervous system damage as abnormalities in reflexes and cranial nerves, lateralized dysfunctions, and the presence of pathologic reflexes. "Soft" signs represented non-localizing evidence of central nervous system dysfunction and included (1) clearly recognizable disturbances of speech, (2) hyperkinesis, (3) failure to maintain balance, (4) disturbances of gait, (5) inadequacies of muscle tone, (6) coordination defects, and (7) extinction to criterion in response to double simultaneous tactile stimulation.

The design and scoring of the neurologic examination resulted in four types of findings on the basis of which to classify the mentally subnormal children. The types of findings noted were (1) the absence of any abnormal neurologic signs, (2) the presence of signs of peripheral nerve damage, as in brachial plexus palsy, (3) the presence of localizing ("hard") signs of central nervous system damage, and (4) the presence of non-localizing ("soft") signs of central nervous system dysfunction. Children with any localizing signs of central nervous system damage as well as children with two non-localizing signs or more were classed as CNS+, a designation indicating the clinical judgment that the child had central nervous system damage. Children without any abnormal neurologic signs, as well as those either with evidence of peripheral nerve lesions only or with fewer than two non-localizing abnormal signs, were classified as CNS−, a designation indicating that, in clinical judgment, insufficient evidence existed for concluding that the child had a damaged brain. The scheme of classification may be summarized as follows:

CNS+	CNS−
1. Any localizing sign of CNS damage.	1. No abnormal signs.
2. Two non-localizing signs or more of CNS damage.	2. Fewer than two non-localizing signs of CNS damage.
3. Both localizing and non-localizing signs of CNS damage.	3. Signs of peripheral nerve injury.

Because of certain widely prevalent misconceptions about the logic of interpreting findings on clinical neurologic evaluation, it is necessary to introduce a precautionary note before presenting the findings. It must be recognized that, when there are sufficient findings of abnormality on clinical neurologic examination, the presence of an organic defect in brain may, with confidence, be judged to be present. However, although it is parsimonious to assume so, this evaluation by no means provides proof positive that the mental subnormality was "caused" by the damage. Moreover, as Masland (1963) has noted, a converse conclusion is not warranted and "Failure to demonstrate an anatomic defect should not be considered as proof that no such defect exists. It may be that even minor variations in the number or the arrangement of the cellular elements of the brain may influence intelligence. Evaluation of such variations has never been undertaken on a systematic scale" (p. 294).

With these strictures in mind we can now turn to the findings on central nervous system damage in the sample of mentally subnormal children.

Findings on Neurologic Evaluation. The overall evaluation of clinical neurologic status in the mentally subnormal children studied is summarized by sex in Table 6. As may be seen from these data, 50, or 49 percent, of the mentally subnormal children examined were found to have clear signs of central nervous system pathology. Of

TABLE 6.

Clinical neurologic status of mentally subnormal children

| Sex | No. of Children with Signs* | | | | | |
| | CNS+ | | | CNS− | | |
	"Hard"	"Soft"	Total	None	Peripheral	Total
Male............	16	13	29	24	2	26
Female.........	11	10	21	21	4	25
Total..........	27	23	50	45	6	51

* Not examined: 2 males; 1 female.

TABLE 7.

Relation of severity of intellectual handicap to clinical neurologic findings*

| IQ Level | No. of Children with Neurologic Status | |
	CNS+	CNS−
<60	36	13
≧60	14	38

* $\chi^2 = 20.042$; $p < 0.001$.

these, approximately equal numbers had "hard" localizing signs and "soft" signs indicative of organic brain dysfunction. In addition, among the cases that were rated as CNS−, six of the children—four girls and two boys—had evidence of peripheral nerve damage. No significant sex differences were found with respect to the relative frequency with which evidence of central nervous system damage was associated with mental subnormality, and sexes are combined in subsequent analyses.

The findings of central nervous system damage were not randomly distributed over the whole range of intellect in the mentally subnormal children but were most frequently found in those children with the lowest IQs. If the group is divided at the median IQ of 60, it may be seen in Table 7 and Figure 2 that the clinical finding of central nervous system abnormality was significantly more frequent in mentally subnormal children with IQs below 60 than in children with IQs above this level. Three times as many of the children with IQs below 60 had clear evidence of neurologic disorder on clinical examination than was the case for mentally subnormal children with IQs equal to or greater than 60. The difference in the frequency with which clinical neurologic findings were noted at the two IQ levels was significant and indicated a stronger association of central nervous system damage with lower IQ.

Clinical Assessment of Psychiatric Status

Psychiatric status was the third feature of current functioning to be evaluated in the course of the clinical assessment of the mentally subnormal children. This aspect of clinical assessment was carried out because (1) at various times psychiatric abnormality has been advanced as an important cause of mental subnormality (Beier, 1964; Garfield, 1963; Sarason & Gladwin, 1958), and (2) the effective management and planning of services for mentally subnormal children, as well as etiologic concerns, require knowledge of the frequency with which behavioral disorders are associated with mental subnormality, the degree of severity of intellectual impairment most likely to be associated with psychiatric abnormality, and the differential rate of such an association in various segments of the population. At present our knowledge in relation to any of these questions is sparse and, as Beier (p. 458, 1964) has put it in his comprehensive review, "No projections can be made for any general populations, since the subjects of these surveys have already been selected or segregated by special psychological, legal, social

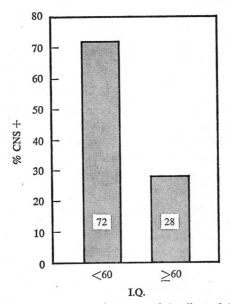

Figure 2. Central nervous system damage and intellectual level in mentally subnormal children.

or economic factors and are, therefore, not representative of more general populations."

Our psychiatric assessment was designed to identify those children who exhibited behavioral abnormalities over and above those limitations in adaptive capacity normally expected to attend a given degree of severity of intellectual handicap. The evaluation was based on historical information about the child's behavior obtained by interviewing his teacher and/or caretaker, on observation of the child and, where, as was the case in most instances, the child was sufficiently responsive, on an individual diagnostic interview of the child himself.

In the course of interviews and observations, the psychiatrist sought to elicit information on the child's behavior in relation to peers and adults, to assess the quality of his relatedness to other persons and to his general environment, to evaluate the appropriateness of his responsiveness to demands for functioning in social situations, to explore his qualities of mood and emotionality, to estimate his assertiveness or degree of withdrawal, to evaluate language and speech organization, to determine activity level with particular attention paid to signs of hypo- or hyperkinesis, to note manifestations of diminished attention span or easy distractibility, and to assess manifestations of aggression. In addition, specific neurotic behaviors, such as phobic reactions, mannerisms, and unusual manifestations of anxiety, were noted.

All children were seen and assessed, and in all cases the interviews and observations were carried out by the same child psychiatrist. He constantly sought to evaluate his findings in light of the child's intellectual level and judged a behavior as being psychiatrically abnormal only when it was clearly excessive after due allowance had been made for the fact and degree of the child's mental subnormality. Such a judgment was, of course, always clinical and subjective but, within these limits, it represented a fair estimate of psychiatric abnormality.

Findings on Psychiatric Evaluation. The data obtained from direct examination, observation, and interview were assimilated to a single record form (*cf.* Appendix 4) and *in toto* constituted the basis for an assignment for the child to one of three psychiatric categories: (1) abnormal, (2) questionably abnormal, or (3) normal. All children studied were assigned to one of these categories and the results of such classification are presented in Table 8. As may be seen from this table, onehalf of the children were found to have no significant psychiatric abnormalities. Of the remainder, in the psychiatrist's judgment, 30 percent were clearly aberrant in their behavior and 20 percent were borderline

TABLE 8.

Psychiatric status of mentally subnormal children

Psychiatric Status	No. of Children			
	Male	Female	Total	Percent
Normal.............	28	24	52	50
Abnormal..........	15	16	31	30
Uncertain.........	13	8	21	20

TABLE 9.

*Relation of psychiatric status to IQ level in mentally subnormal children**

IQ Level	No. of Children with Psychiatric Status		
	Abnormal	Normal	Total
<50	14	13	27
50–59	10	3	13
Total	24	16	40
60–69	5	16	21
≧70	2	20	22
Total	7	36	43

* $\chi^2 = 15.11$; $p < 0.001$.

cases who were questionably normal. No sex differences were found on psychiatric evaluation.

As may be seen in Table 9 and Figure 3, abnormal behavior was strongly and positively associated with the degree of severity of mental subnormality. In children whose IQs were below 60, almost one-half were psychiatrically abnormal. Of the remainder, 40 percent were rated as doubtfully abnormal and 60 percent, as normal. In contrast, relatively few of the mentally subnormal children with an IQ of 60 or above were judged to be psychiatrically abnormal, with only 18 percent of the remainder judged as doubtfully abnormal. The association of psychiatric abnormality and low IQ level was strong.

As may be seen from Table 10 and Figure 4, psychiatric abnormality also had a significant and positive association with the presence of central nervous system damage. Whereas a majority of the mentally subnormal children judged to be psychiatrically normal had no clinical findings of central nervous system damage, the children who were judged to be psychiatrically abnormal had a high frequency of such findings.

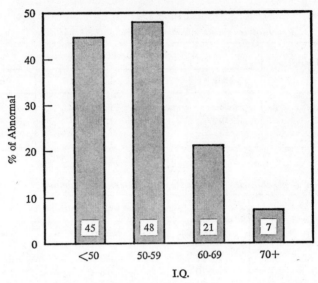

Figure 3. Psychiatric status and intellectual level in mentally subnormal children.

TABLE 10.

*Relation of psychiatric status to neurologic status
in mentally subnormal children**

Neurologic Status	No. of Children with Psychiatric Status	
	Abnormal	Normal
CNS+	21	20
CNS−	10	30

*$\chi^2 = 4.834$; $p < 0.05$.

Since the judgment of neurologic abnormality included children with both "hard" and "soft" signs of central nervous system dysfunction, it is of value to consider the association of psychiatric abnormality with each of these indices of dysfunction separately. When this analysis is made (Table 11 and Figure 5), only a weak and non-significant positive association is obtained between psychiatric abnormality and the presence of "hard" signs of central nervous system dysfunction. However, the association between the findings of "soft" neurologic signs and the judgment of abnormality in psychiatric status

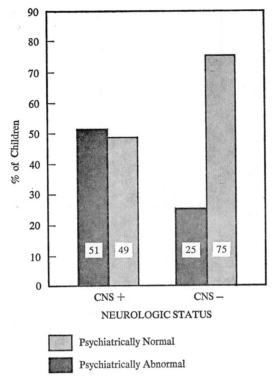

Figure 4. Psychiatric abnormality and clinical neurologic status in mentally subnormal children.

TABLE 11.

*Relation of psychiatric status to type of neurologic abnormality**

Signs of Central Nervous System Damage	No. of Children with Psychiatric Status	
	Normal	Abnormal
"Soft"	7	12
None	30	10

* $\chi^2 = 6.471$; p $<$ 0.02.

is strong and the relation is positive. This finding is of particular interest, since in this study abnormalities of attitude and behavior as such were not used as "soft" signs of central nervous system damage.

Since the signs of both neurologic damage and abnormal psychiatric

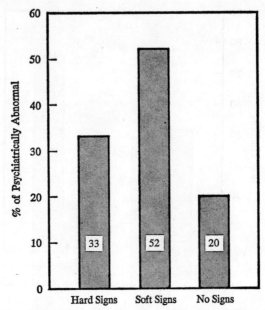

Figure 5. The relation of psychiatric abnormality to "hard" and "soft" neurologic signs of central nervous system damage.

status were more prevalent in the children with lower IQs, it was possible that the obtained association between the two measures derived from their common existence in the most severely impaired mentally subnormal children. An analysis of this possibility indicated that this is, indeed, the case and that, whereas a positive association exists between "soft" signs of central nervous system dysfunction and psychiatric abnormality among the children of lower IQ, no such relation obtains for the children whose mental subnormality is of lesser degrees of severity (Table 12).

The relationships among the three clinical variables and the patterning of clinical characteristics in the mentally subnormal children are summarized in Table 13 and are represented graphically in Figure 6. Clearly, associated neurologic or psychiatric findings are most manifest in cases of more severe mental subnormality. Conversely, the absence of such associations tends to characterize mental subnormality of mild degree.

The Social Distribution of Degrees of Mental Subnormality

Having defined certain of the clinical features of mental subnormality, we may now return to the aspect of prevalence that was deferred

TABLE 12.

Relation of psychiatric status to "soft" signs of neurologic damage and IQ

Neurologic Status and IQ Level	No. of Children with Psychiatric Status	
	Abnormal	Normal
"Soft" signs present		
IQ < 60	9	1
IQ ≧ 60	2	6

TABLE 13.

Patterning of clinical signs of dysfunction

Pattern	No. of Children	Prevalance per 1000
IQ ≧ 60 only...	33	4.00
IQ ≧ 60 and CNS+.................................	12	1.45
IQ ≧ 60 and psychiatric abnormality.................	5	0.61
IQ ≧ 60, CNS+, and psychiatric abnormality.........	2	0.24
IQ < 60 only...	8	0.97
IQ < 60 and CNS+.................................	17	2.05
IQ < 60 and psychiatric abnormality.................	5	0.61
IQ < 60, CNS+, and psychiatric abnormality.........	19	2.30
Total...	101	

in Chapter 3 until these features had been delineated—the relation of prevalence of mental subnormality to social class. In particular we will consider at this point two aspects of this problem: (1) the overall relation of mental subnormality to social class, and (2) the social class distribution of different degrees of severity of mental subnormality.

The prevalence of mental subnormality was lowest in the upper social classes (I to IIIa) and, for each step downward in social class, prevalence increased by a factor of 2 (Table 14). The prevalence of mental subnormality in the lowest social class (V) was nine times higher than the prevalence in the upper social classes (I to IIIa). In comparison with the prevalence rate of 12.6 per 1000 for all social classes combined, Social Classes I to IIIa and IIIb are underrepresented, whereas Social Class V is heavily overrepresented.

The determination of the relation of social class to the prevalence of different degrees of severity of mental subnormality was carried out

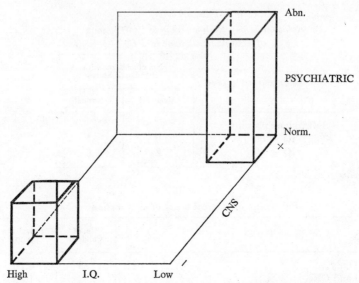

Figure 6. The interrelations of IQ, psychiatric abnormality, and clinical signs of central nervous system damage in the mentally subnormal population.

in two steps. First, the mentally subnormal children were divided into two groups around the median IQ score of 60 and second, since an IQ of less than 50 has been widely used to separate "educable" from "trainable" mentally subnormal children, the group with IQs of less than 60 was again divided so that the children with IQs below 50 were separated from those with IQs of 50 to 59. These divisions resulted in three IQ ranges for the classification of the children in terms of the severity of their mental handicap:

$$IQ = 60 \text{ and above}$$
$$IQ = 50 \text{ to } 59$$
$$IQ = \text{below } 50.$$

The social class distribution of the mentally subnormal children by these three ranges of IQ is presented in Table 15 and Figure 7. From this table it is clear that the high prevalence of mental subnormality in the lower social classes derives very largely from the excess of cases with IQ above 60. For this level of impairment, prevalence increases in a step-wise progression as we go down the social scale from a low of 0 in the highest social class to 24.9 per 1000 in Social Class V. The gradient is present for IQ 50 to 59 but is weaker. Strikingly, the most severe level of intellectual impairment exhibits no prevalence gradient. It is of

TABLE 14.

Social class distribution of mentally subnormal children

Social Class	No. of Children in Population*	No. of Mentally Subnormal Children	Prevalence of Mental Subnormality per 1000
I–IIIa	2405	9	3.7
IIIb	1904	16	8.4
IIIc	1648	26	15.8
IV	1087	19	17.5
V	1044	34	32.6
N.R.†	186	0	—
Total	8274	104	12.6

* The figures indicate the total number of children of the age range in each social class.

† N.R., not reported.

TABLE 15.

Prevalence of differing degrees of severity of mental subnormality by social class

Social Class	No. of Children in Population	No. and Prevalence Rate per 1000 of Mentally Subnormal Children at IQ Level					
		<50		50–59		≧60	
		No.	Prevalence	No.	Prevalence	No.	Prevalence
I–IIIa	2405	8	3.3	1	0.4	0	0
IIIb	1904	7	3.7	6	3.1	3	1.6
IIIc	1648	10	6.1	6	3.6	10	6.1
IV	1087	3	2.8	3	2.8	13	11.9
V	1044	3	2.9	5	4.8	26	24.9
Total	8088	31	3.8	21	2.6	52	6.4

interest to note, too, that there is so little mild subnormality among the children whose fathers are in the non-manual classes (I to IIIa).

A somewhat different viewpoint of the social class prevalence of mental subnormality is obtained if one focuses on the distribution of degrees of severity of mental subnormality *within* any social class rather than on differences *between* social classes. As may be seen in Figure 8, there are 0 percent of children in Social Classes I to IIIa who are mildly subnormal, but 76 per cent of the subnormal children in Social Class V are of this type. Conversely, 89 percent of the mentally subnormal children in Social Classes I to IIIa have IQs of less than 50, whereas only 9 percent are found in Social Class V. Thus, if a child is mentally subnormal, the likelihood of his having an IQ of less than 50

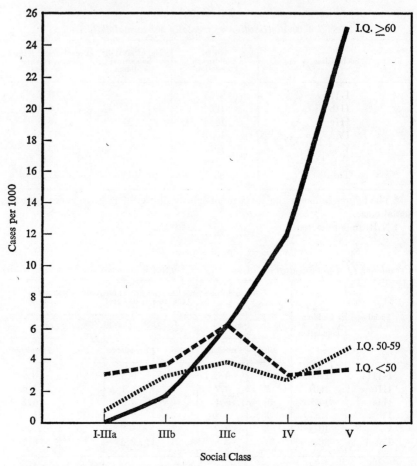

Figure 7. The prevalence of different levels of IQ in the mentally subnormal children in different social classes.

is 10 times greater if he belongs to Social Classes I to IIIa than it is if he is in Social Class V.

It was possible, of course, that the marked elevation of prevalence for mild subnormality in the lower social classes was the result of social class bias in the ascertainment of children with IQs between 60 and 75, as was noted in Chapter 3. Such an elevation in prevalence could have occurred if the educational and health authorities systematically noted children at borderline levels of IQ as mentally subnormal if they came from lower social class families but failed to do so if they came from upper social class families. To explore this possibility, we analyzed the

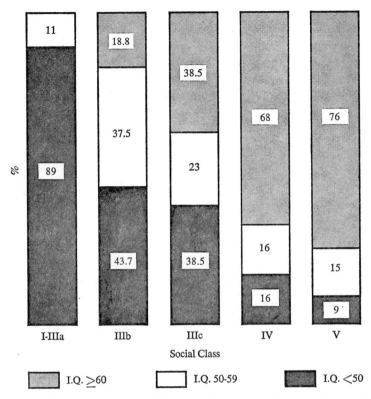

Figure 8. The percentage of children having various degrees of severity of mental subnormality in each social class.

social class composition of the 123 children described in Chapter 3 who scored below 75 on the screening test at age 7 and were thus at risk of being classified as mentally subnormal but whom the educational authorities had not so classified (Table 16).

It is clear from these data that the children who, on psychometric evaluation, had an IQ of 75 or less but were not administratively ascertained as mentally subnormal show the same general social class prevalence distribution as do the administratively defined cases, with increases in prevalence at every step down the social class scale, epitomized by Social Class V, which has a prevalence more than six times as great as do Social Classes I to IIIa. If these cases were added to the 104 cases that had been administratively classified as mentally subnormal, no change in the prevalence gradient would result. The social distribution of mental subnormality indicates that the dysfunction is

TABLE 16.

Social class prevalence of children in ordinary schools but with psychometric score of less than 75 on test taken at age 7

Social Class	No. of Children in Population	No. and Prevalence per 1000 of Children in Ordinary Schools with IQ Scores <75	
		No.	Prevalence
I–IIIa	2405	8	3.3
IIIb	1904	24	12.6
IIIc	1648	30	18.2
IV	1087	22	20.2
V	1044	34	32.6
X*	?	5	—
Total		123	

* X, Illegitimate children.

overrepresented in the lower social classes and underrepresented in the upper social classes. Moreover, the overrepresentation of mental subnormality in the lower social classes is accounted for almost entirely by an excess of children with mild or borderline subnormality, while most severe degrees of subnormality are not systematically associated with social class.

Earlier studies of the social class distribution of mental subnormality based upon (1) populations in residential institutions, (2) backward children in the schools, and (3) surveys of mental subnormality in cities or other geographically defined areas are in general accord with our findings. Hilliard and Kirman (1957) have reported the distribution by social class of all patients under 16 years of age admitted to mental deficiency hospitals in England and Wales in the 2-year period 1950 to 1951 and have found that children of parents with unskilled manual occupations were more often admitted to the hospitals than would be expected from the prevalence of such children in the total population. Conversely, children from the upper social classes were admitted less often than would be expected. More recent studies of mental deficiency institutions in England (Penrose, 1963) and in the U.S.A. have confirmed these findings and, in addition, have indicated that the children with fathers in the lower socio-economic groups contributed substantially more cases to the number of less severe forms of subnormality than did those with fathers whose occupations were higher on the socio-economic scale.

Burt (1937) studied educational backwardness in children who had been retained in the regular schools and found that more than 20

percent of the children in the poor districts of London were educationally backward, as contrasted with 1 percent in well-to-do neighbor-
hoods. The overall correlation between backwardness and poverty was
0.727 and between backwardness and crowded living conditions, 0.890.
O'Connor (1958), reporting a study in Glasgow which "used the provision of free milk . . . as a measure of poverty and malnutrition," indicated "a positive relationship . . . between the backwardness in schools
in the different areas and the percentage of free milk issued in these
areas . . ." (p. 26, Clarke & Clarke, 1958). McGehee and Lewis (1942)
examined the occupations of the fathers of 45,000 children in the fourth
through eighth grades who were in the highest and lowest 10 percent
of intelligence test scores. For the lowest 10 percent of the children,
who were all in regular schools, 1.5 times as many as expected came
from the lowest social class, whereas 0.14 times as many as expected
derived from the highest social class. These studies suggest that more
children of borderline subnormality come from poverty areas within
a community than come from wealthier areas.

The third type of research relevant to the social distribution of
mental subnormality is illustrated by the Onondaga County study
carried out by the Mental Health Research Unit of the New York State
Department of Mental Hygiene (1955). It provided more direct evidence on the social class distribution of mental subnormality within a
community. In the city of Syracuse, census tracts with populations of
low economic status produced more than their share of children suspected or known to be mentally subnormal. Moreover, higher prevalence rates were found in deteriorating sections of the community (p.
280, Gruenberg, 1964). Prevalence rates of mental retardation by socio-
economic areas for the city of Syracuse, presented in the preliminary
report, showed an almost four-fold increase in the rate from the highest
to the lowest socio-economic area.

The Onondaga study needs to be interpreted cautiously since case
finding included all suspected as well as all known cases and 69 percent
of the children included attended regular classes in public or parochial
schools (p. 107, New York State Department of Mental Hygiene, 1955).
Criteria used for suspicion of mental subnormality are not reported but
undoubtedly included a melange of educational backwardness, behavioral problems, and physical handicaps, as well as more direct evidence of mental incapacity as such.

A similar social class gradient for mild degrees of mental subnormality has been reported for Salford and Manchester by Stein and
Susser (1963, 1967).

Despite the variation in the children studied in each location and in the methods employed, there is general agreement among the earlier studies and between them and the present Aberdeen study that mental subnormality occurs with greatest frequency in the lower social class segments of the community. The suggestion from earlier studies that elevated prevalence in these social groups is largely accounted for by a heavy overrepresentation of mild subnormality is strongly confirmed by the Aberdeen results.

Summary

Viewed as a whole, the examination of current intellectual, neurologic, and psychiatric status in all of the mentally subnormal children between 8 and 10 years of age in the city of Aberdeen, Scotland, has resulted in the following findings:

1. Within the framework of a mental subnormality rate of 12.6 per 1000, 71 percent of the children were at or above 50 in IQ and the remainder were below that level;

2. Significantly more boys than girls were subnormal with IQs of 70 and above;

3. One-half of the children were noted, on independently conducted neurologic examination, to have definite signs of neurologic damage;

4. Psychiatric abnormalities were judged to be definitely present in 30 percent and questionably or uncertainly present in 20 percent of the mentally subnormal children;

5. A strong set of associations existed among the three measures of current functioning, with positive findings of both central nervous system abnormality and abnormality in psychiatric status highly associated with the more severe degrees of intellectual handicap;

6. No significant associations among the clinical measures were noted in children with lesser degrees of intellectual deficit;

7. An analysis of IQ level by social class indicated that: a. there is a significant excess of mildly subnormal children contributed by the lower social classes; b. no social class gradient exists for the prevalence of mental subnormality characterized by an IQ of less than 50; and c. mild degrees of mental subnormality are markedly underrepresented in the upper social classes.

Part Two

THE ETIOLOGY OF
MENTAL SUBNORMALITY

5

The Search for "Cause"

Having defined the prevalence of mental subnormality and certain of its clinical features, we can now turn to the problem of cause. This analysis is not an easy task since "at any given time, an individual's intellectual ability is the end result of the interaction of three factors—the inherited constitution and capability of the nervous system, modification or injury of this structure by prenatal or postnatal injury or disease, and the conditioning or training of the intellect by environmental experiences" (p. 290, Masland, 1963). Consequently, in seeking to identify causes for mental subnormality we must be concerned with the contributions made by heredity, with the physical environment of the embryo, fetus, and child, and with the social and psychologic environment. Moreover, since mental development is always the end result of the interrelations between an individual of given constitution and the particular type of physical and social environment to which he has been exposed, any analysis of cause would be incomplete if the interaction between organismic and environmental variables were not considered.

It is of some value to consider the causal factors noted by Masland as representing two sets of variables—the first, *endogenous* and the second, *exogenous*. The endogenous set embraces genetic factors and inherited constitution, and the exogenous set comprises physical, biologic, and social influences.

Specific genetic abnormalities that have been implicated as causes for mental subnormality are numerous (*cf.* Carter, 1966) and the number of such causes identified increases steadily with improvements in methods for biochemical, clinical, and karyosomal investigation. One variant, as in Down's Syndrome (mongolism), involves an abnormal chromosome number or pattern which is produced either as a consequence of a carrier state in the parents or as an effect produced by maternal aging. The chromosomal abnormality, through mechanisms that are still unclear, results in a genetically atypical organism which, among its other peculiarities, usually exhibits a severe degree of mental subnormality.

A second type of genetic abnormality resulting in mental subnormality is represented by enzymatic aberrations such as have been identified in phenylpyruvic oligophrenia (Jervis, 1959) and maple sugar disease (Dancis, 1959). In such disorders the primary consequence of the abnormal gene structure is the production of abnormal metabolites which function either directly or indirectly to interfere with the development of the central nervous system. Mental subnormality resulting from such disorders is, again, usually of severe degree.

Other specific types of less well-understood genetic abnormalities associated with structural defects and mental subnormality could be mentioned; however, they are rare diseases and, taken together with the enzymatic disorders already noted, probably contribute to fewer than 3 percent of all cases of mental subnormality.

The endogenous explanation that has been applied to the largest number of cases is the concept of a gene pool for intellectual incompetence. It is a view that has been derived from the so-called "normal" curve of intelligence (*cf.* Gruenberg, 1958, for a criticism of this theory) and argues that a certain proportion of cases of low IQ are to be expected in any population on genetic grounds. It notes the distributions of families, sibships, and twinships at various regions on this curve and, from the patterns obtained, argues for a familial and heritable variety of adaptive incompetence underlain by an as yet undefined system or systems of genetic determinants (Zigler, 1967).

The exogenous set of etiologies is a "mixed bag" containing both biologic and social variables. These range from injury or maldevelopment of the fetus because of suboptimal conditions *in utero* to mental incompetence deriving from social circumstances which deprive the child of experiences, values, and attitudes deemed to be essential for his normal intellectual growth. In an extreme form, concern with exogenous contributions to mental subnormality is epitomized by Knobloch and Pasamanick (1959) when they state that "all men are conceived equal" and become aberrant as a consequence of pathogenic influences brought to bear upon them from the outside. Following conception, embryos of presumably equal potentiality may be insulted or facilitated in their development by influences acting upon them *in utero*, at any subsequent point in development, or by some combination of both. These influences may be biologic, as in preeclamptic toxemia and asphyxia; physical, as in exposure to x-irradiation; social, as in the case of individuals subjected to deprived, defective, or distorted bodies of experience or motivation; or clearly biosocial, as in the associations of poverty, maternal ill health, malnutrition, and stunting.

In analyzing our data for the purpose of defining "causes" for mental subnormality, we will relate our findings to this general etiologic scheme. The method to be used in doing so is perhaps best defined as *an accountability analysis*. Such an analysis is in essence a step-wise process of exclusion through which "cause" remains to be assigned to an ever smaller residuum of cases.

The first step in the analysis consists of identifying those cases in the mentally subnormal group who can most readily be accounted for in terms of an underlying defect. These are the cases with Down's Syndrome. For these cases we argue that since clear evidence of a specific chromosomal abnormality and of structural abnormality exists (Penrose & Smith, 1967), such evidence, in and of itself, is sufficient to account for the fact of mental subnormality. Once such a cause is assigned, the cases so identified are excluded from subsequent etiologic analysis. In the present series of cases, five children were identified as mongols and were so accounted for.*

The next step in the analysis was the identification of any cases in which there was clear evidence of neoplastic processes, trauma, or infection of the central nervous system resulting in mental subnormality. In our series there was one instance of such a case—a boy with a clear history of normal motor, adaptive, and intellectual development to the age of 2 years 10 months when, following a bout of severe meningoencephalitis, he was postencephalitic and manifested persistent signs of subnormal mental functioning.

The third step is to argue that when mental subnormality is of severe degree and when mental subnormality of any degree is accompanied by clear clinical findings of central nervous system damage, such damage is considered sufficient to account for the fact of subnormality on neurologic grounds. Thus, all children with IQs of less than 50 and all mentally subnormal children classified as CNS+ are cases in which the mental subnormality is viewed to be, at least

---

* A similar process of accountability would have been applied to identified cases of enzymatic or genetic defect, but the absence of data necessary for such an analysis made this impossible in the series studied.

in part, a consequence of insult or injury to the central nervous system. Clearly, the obverse is not true, and one cannot argue that the absence of neurologic findings may be used as a basis for assuming the absence of damage to the nervous system since, as has already been noted (*cf.* Chapter 4), the clinical neurologic examination is sufficiently insensitive to permit a high frequency of false negative findings. Rather, the absence of clinical evidence of central nervous system damage leaves the question of etiology open and leads to the fourth step in the analysis.

This step is a complex one which seeks to assess the etiologic contributions of familial factors as well as of other biologic and social conditions of risk. It involves a comparative analysis of neurologically positive and negative cases in terms of social backgrounds, obstetric experience, perinatal condition, family circumstances, and sibling characteristics, through which we will seek to identify plausible etiologies for the remaining cases. The analysis to be presented in the next four chapters will pursue these objectives and, through a set of clinical and social cross-comparisons, will examine hypotheses relating to the causation of mental subnormality in the sample of mentally subnormal children studied. At each step, too, the interactions among sets of influences will be considered. The findings will serve to establish "guilt by association" and will help to provide inferences about cause that may in their turn be investigated in subsequent *ad hoc* studies.

6

Etiologic Implications of the Social Distribution of Subtypes of Mental Subnormality

In the present chapter we will begin our consideration of etiology in mental subnormality by examining the social class distribution of different subtypes of the dysfunction. Against the background of the findings already reported, we can take our first step in accounting for cause by identifying those children in our population for whom the cause of the impairment has been clearly established. This group consists of five children with Down's Syndrome and one child whose mental subnormality was clearly the consequence of meningoencephalitis in the third year of life. With these cases eliminated from further etiologic concern, there remain 98 cases for whom the cause of mental subnormality is not immediately apparent and remains to be defined. In these cases any one or any combination of the following general factors could have contributed to the handicap:

1. Biologic insults deriving from disordered fetal, perinatal, and postnatal environments;

2. Non-specific genetic or familial factors which result in poor physical and mental development;

3. Social disadvantages which prevent the full development of intellectual functioning.

As we have already noted (Chapter 4), the least severely impaired of the mentally subnormal children were most frequently found in the lowest social class. In contrast, cases with the most severe degrees of impairment were randomly distributed across social classes. We shall concern ourselves first with those mentally subnormal children having IQs of less than 50 and clear clinical evidence of central nervous system damage. For such children there are sound grounds (both of parsimony in interpretation and in the clinical neurologic findings of brain damage) for deciding that the mental subnormality derived primarily from central nervous system damage. Moreover, our finding that these severely mentally subnormal children are randomly distributed across social classes (Table 1) provides no reasonable basis for inferring that social-environmental or familial-constitutional factors had made a significant contribution to the production of the handicap. Following this line of reasoning permits us to assign brain damage as the major cause for mental subnormality in 23 children who had IQs of less than 50 and clinical evidence of central nervous system damage.

We are left, therefore, with 75 children—one with an IQ of less than 50* and the remainder having IQs of 50 or greater—for whom an etiology remains to be assigned. We shall deal first with those children in the group with IQs above 50 who have associated findings of central nervous system damage. The distribution of these children by social class is presented in Table 2. As may be noted, 25 of the children with IQs equal to or greater than 50 had clinical evidence of central nervous system damage. Such cases were not randomly distributed by social class but had their greatest relative frequency in the lowest social class, where the actual number of cases was almost four times as great as that which could have been expected by chance alone. In contrast, only one case of this type was in the upper social class grouping and, for this class, the actual frequency was one-seventh of the frequency that could have been expected by chance. Thus, the prevalence in Social Class V for this subvariant of mental subnormality was 25 times greater than for Social Classes I to IIIa. These findings suggest either that an IQ of 50 or greater deriving from biologic insult is less frequent in the highest social class grouping or that given levels of biologic insult interact with different social-environmental and familial conditions to produce significant subnormality in socially deprived individuals and have little effect on the socially advantaged individuals.

We are now left with 48 cases† with IQs of 50 or greater without clinical evidence of central nervous system damage for whom no pre-

---

* There was no clinical evidence of central nervous system damage in this case and, for the sake of simplicity in analysis, it was excluded from consideration.

† There was no information on central nervous system damage for one of the cases with IQ of 50 or greater—hence, this figure instead of 49.

TABLE 1.

Social class distribution of mentally subnormal children with IQ < 50 and clinical evidence of central nervous system damage

Social Class	No. of Children in Population	Actual No. Mentally Subnormal	Expected No. Mentally Subnormal*	Actual No./ Expected No.†
I–IIIa	2405	7	6.80	1.03
IIIb	1904	4	5.41	0.74
IIIc	1648	6	4.70	1.28
IV	1087	3	3.10	0.97
V	1044	3	2.90	1.03
Total	8088	23		1.00

* (Total at risk in social class) × (Total mentally subnormal < 50 with central nervous system damage)/Total at risk in total population.

† A figure greater than 1.0 indicates a higher concentration and a figure less than 1.0 indicates a lower concentration of cases than expected.

TABLE 2.

Social class distribution of mentally subnormal children with IQ ≥ 50 and clinical evidence of central nervous system damage

Social Class	No. of Children in Population	Actual No. Mentally Subnormal	Expected No. Mentally Subnormal	Actual No./ Expected No.
I–IIIa	2405	1	7.40	0.14
IIIb	1904	6	5.90	1.01
IIIc	1648	4	5.10	0.78
IV	1087	2	3.40	0.60
V	1044	12	3.20	3.80
Total	8088	25		

sumptive etiology can readily be assigned. Our present state of knowledge precludes a confident assignment of accountability for cause to any of the general causal factors previously listed, and it is perhaps for this reason that the literature abounds in diverse opinions about etiology for this subtype of mental subnormality.

The central difficulty in determining cause for this subtype lies in the absence of clinical evidence of central nervous system damage. Without such evidence, we can approach the problem of cause only by indirect analysis and by inferential methods.

The absence of data on genetic and enzymatic causes, except for Down's Syndrome, makes it impossible to consider these causes in this study. Further, although the possibility of central nervous system insult undetected by clinical neurologic examination is an interesting mechanism about which to speculate, it is in fact unexaminable in our sample. We are left, therefore, with only two possibilities for pursuing accountability—constitutional factors and social-familial environment. In the present study there is no way in which we can separate these factors in terms of relative contribution to cause.

The social class distribution of the mentally subnormal children in the group with IQs of 50 and greater and with no evidence of central nervous system damage is presented in Table 3. These data reveal a marked social class gradient, beginning with a total absence of cases in Social Classes I to IIIa and a step-wise increase in prevalence down the social class scale until a prevalence that is three times greater than expectancy is found in Social Class V. This finding supports the inference that social-environmental and familial factors are contributing to cause in this subtype of mental subnormality.

Further evidence in support of this view is obtained from an examination of those cases whose intellectual impairment is least severe—that is, those with IQs of 60 or greater. As may be noted in Table 4, none of these cases occurs in the upper two social class groupings and, in the middle grouping, the number of cases is almost exactly equal to chance expectancy. However, in Social Classes IV and V, the number of cases is respectively 2.4 and 3.7 times greater than would have been expected by chance alone. It is possible that the heavy representation of these cases found in the lower social classes and the complete absence of such cases in the two upper social class groupings could have derived from selection biases by social class in the identification of mildly subnormal children. This possibility may be considered by examining the children who may be designated as

TABLE 3.

Social class distribution of mentally subnormal children with IQ $\geq$ 50 without clinical signs of central nervous system damage

Social Class	No. of Children in Population	Actual No. Mentally Subnormal	Expected No. Mentally Subnormal	Actual No./ Expected No.
I–IIIa	2405	0	14.30	0
IIIb	1904	3	11.30	0.27
IIIc	1648	12	9.80	1.22
IV	1087	14	6.50	2.20
V	1044	19	6.20	3.10
Total	8088	48		

TABLE 4.

Social class distribution of mentally subnormal children with $IQ \geqq 60$ without clinical evidence of central nervous system damage

Social Class	No. of Children in Population	Actual No. Mentally Subnormal	Expected No. Mentally Subnormal	Actual No./ Expected No.
I–IIIa	2405	0	11.3	0
IIIb	1904	0	8.9	0
IIIc	1648	8	7.7	1.0
IV	1087	12	5.1	2.4
V	1044	18	4.9	3.7
Total	8088	38		

TABLE 5.

Social class distribution of children with $IQ < 75$ in regular schools

Social Class	No. of Children in Population	Actual No. Mentally Subnormal	Expected No. Mentally Subnormal	Actual No./ Expected No.
I–IIIa	2405	8	35.1	0.23
IIIb	1904	24	27.8	0.86
IIIc	1648	30	24.0	1.25
IV	1087	22	15.9	1.38
V	1044	34	15.2	2.24
Total	8088	118*		

* Because five of the original population of 123 in this group are in foster homes, social class information was not available for them.

borderline subnormal—*i.e.*, children in regular schools with psychometric ratings of less than 75 on the screening test given to all children at age 7 (Chapter 3). The social class distribution of these children is presented in Table 5. It is clear from these data that, if the psychometric criterion alone had been used for selecting children for special schools, the same general social class gradient would obtain as was noted above. This finding suggests that, although there is some evidence of administrative bias, the overrepresentation of cases found in the lower social classes of our intensively studied sample was not an artifact of selective placement in special schools but a true reflection of the distribution of the phenomenon in the population.

In a sense, these findings reflect certain general tendencies with respect to the distribution of IQ in the community. Many studies (Douglas, 1964; Conant, 1961; Pringle *et al*, 1966; Neff, 1938; Eells *et al*, 1951) have shown that, in general, children whose parents have low income, unskilled manual jobs, and minimal education perform less well in school and on intelligence tests than do children whose parents have higher incomes and are in skilled technical or professional occupations.

In Figure 1 we present the overall distribution by social class of Aberdeen children with test scores between 80 and 109 and, in Figure 2, we show that of children with test scores greater than 120. It may

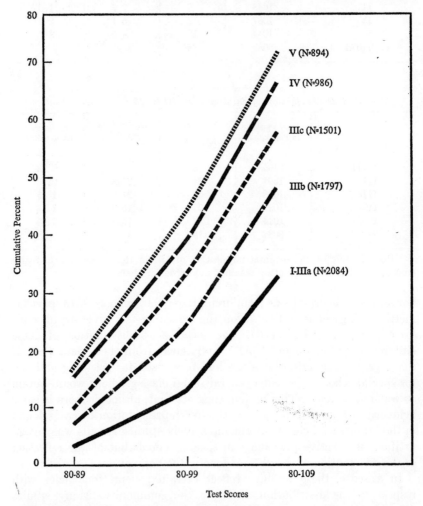

Figure 1. Cumulative percent in each social class of 7+ test scores between 80 and 109 for children born in Aberdeen 1951 to 1955.

be noted in these figures that the percentage of individuals with low scores increases with each downward step in social class and, conversely, that the proportion of children with high IQs increases in a step-wise manner as one progresses up the social class scale. The consistency of these gradients in the total population of children provides indirect support for the inference that social-environmental and familial factors make an important contribution to these mild forms of mental subnormality in which no clinical evidence of central nervous system abnormality is found.

Our search for cause through an examination of the social class distribution of mental subnormality would not be complete without considering the suggestion that the heavy concentration of mental subnormality in the lowest social class could be the result of a highly stable and closely intermarried subpopulation with an inferior genetic endowment for intellectual competence. Although, as was noted earlier, we cannot separate social-environmental from familial factors, we are

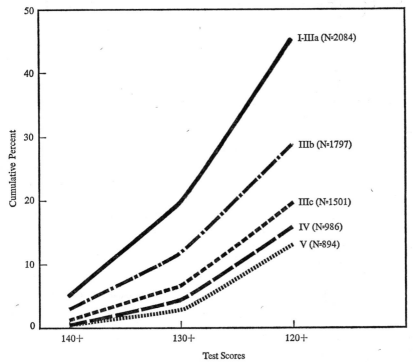

Figure 2. Cumulative percent in each social class of 7+ test scores higher than 120 for children born in Aberdeen 1951 to 1955.

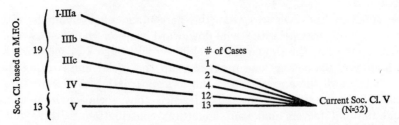

Figure 3. Intergenerational shifts in the social class position of mothers of mentally subnormal children from mother's father's occupation (M.F.O.) to husband's occupation.

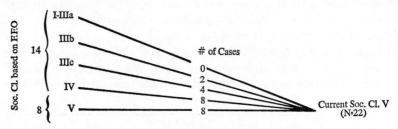

Figure 4. Intergenerational shifts in the social class position of fathers of mentally subnormal children from father's father's occupation (F.F.O.) to father's occupation.

able to examine the integenerational stability of the lowest social class to determine whether this suggestion may be supported. For the mentally subnormal population, information is available not only on the social class of the family in which the child lives but also on the social class of the preceding generation. Figures 3 and 4 show that, of the mothers and fathers of mentally subnormal children currently in Social Class V, only 41 and 36 percent, respectively, were brought up in this social class, the remainder of the parents having been reared in higher social classes. When both parents are considered together, we find that only 23 percent were raised in Social Class V and remained there after marriage and the birth of the mentally subnormal child. This evidence does not support the idea of an inbred and highly stable lowest social class with an inferior genetic endowment but rather suggests the possibility of downward social movement into the lowest social class of some men and women who may provide either a poor endowment or an inadequate environment for the development of their children. In addition, women in this downwardly mobile group may be at greater obstetric risk.

In this chapter we have begun an approach to etiology first by defining those cases in which etiologies are readily identified and then by using social class distributions of clinical subtypes of mental subnormality as a basis for making inferences about cause in the remaining group. In particular, we have inferred primary central nervous system damage to be the most parsimonious explanation for the most severe forms of intellectual handicap and for those cases with intellectual handicap of any degree who have associated clinical findings of central nervous system damage. This argument is, of course, most fully supportable for the first of these two clinical types. Within the second type, for those cases with milder degrees of intellectual handicap, the findings suggest the interaction of biologic insult with social-environmental and familial-constitutional factors as the causal explanation.

We have suggested the existence of social-environmental and/or familial factors as important contributors to cause in those cases with relatively mild intellectual impairment and no clinical evidence of central nervous system insult. In largest part, the inferences that have been made in the course of our analyses have derived from a consideration of the social class distribution of subtypes of mental subnormality. We recognize, however, that social class is only a general indicator of the conditions of life associated with certain occupational categories and that, as Kohn (1963) has stated,

... it refers to more than simply educational level, or occupation, or any of the large number of correlated variables. It is so useful because it captures the reality that the intricate interplay of all these variables creates different basic conditions of life at different levels of the social order. Members of different social classes, by virtue of enjoying (or suffering) different conditions of life, come to see the world differently—to develop different conceptions of social reality, different aspirations and hopes and fears, different conceptions of the desirable.

It is therefore possible that, if the cases in which mild mental subnormality is overrepresented are considered in relation to other social factors, such as family size, organization, and housing, additional information may be obtained about the life circumstances in which there are heightened risks for mental subnormality in the child. This issue will be examined in the following chapter.

7

Family Conditions and Mild Mental Subnormality in the Lower Social Classes

The social class analysis of Chapter 6 is a first step in understanding the relationship between mental subnormality and environmental experience. Our measure of social class was based on the occupation of the child's father, this being perhaps the most effective single criterion available and the one most frequently used in sociomedical research. Like any simple and indirect indicator of a complex phenomenon, occupational class has a limited power of discrimination, since heterogeneity in actual condition of family life characterizes all occupational classes. Some unskilled workers (Social Class V) provide their children with a material and cultural environment equivalent to that of Social Class III children, while the highly heterogeneous Social Class III contains within itself subgroups akin at one end to Social Classes I and II and at the other end to Social Classes IV and V. It is necessary, therefore, to analyze other indicators of family circumstances and social, cultural, and economic experience in Social Classes IV and V. Our purpose in this chapter is to examine a number of such indicators. Our knowledge of the child's environmental circumstances clearly is increased if, in addition to the father's occupation, we know whether the mother is professionally qualified, a clerical worker, or a manual worker, and whether the family lives in a middle class district or an area of old, dilapidated, and overcrowded houses.*

The criteria used in this further analysis are largely sociodemographic in nature—mother's premarital occupation, size of family, area of residence, and degree of crowding. These criteria are used to identify

---

* Level of education was not used because almost all mothers in these social classes left school at the age permitted by law.

social subgroups in which mental subnormality occurs most frequently, our premise being that a more precise identification and definition of such subgroups may lead to fruitful inferences about causation. While our indicators may identify social groups with a high prevalence of mental subnormality, the indicators themselves may be causally unimportant. The significant experiences of the child within these groups will be something that our variables reflect only indirectly, *e.g.*, the linguistic behavior of such groups, their modes of thought and explanation, or their perception of their own ability to participate in the educational, occupational, and social activities of a wider society. Nor does high prevalence in a socially defined group rule out the possibility of biologic defect, for it may well be that children in such groups are particularly subject to biologic insult prenatally, at delivery, or in childhood.

Because we are looking for those subgroups in which socially influenced subnormality is most likely, we have limited the scope of analysis in this chapter to a population defined by two variables: (1) children in Social Classes IV and V, which were shown in the previous chapter to have the highest incidence of mental subnormality, and (2) children with an IQ of 60 or greater and with no clinical evidence of central nervous system damage—this being the subtype of mental subnormality which is most clearly overrepresented in the lowest social classes and the one in which social experience has been assumed to be a primary cause (Penrose, 1963; Sarason & Gladwin, 1958; Zigler, 1967).

We have also undertaken a comparable analysis of the family characteristics of children who are in regular schools but who had intelligence test scores of less than 75 on the test given at age 7. These borderline subnormal children may provide additional useful evidence in our inquiry since, in both their level of intellectual development and their social class distribution, they bear a closer resemblance to the minimally subnormal children than to the general population of children who are not mentally subnormal.

If families with certain social characteristics have a high prevalence of mild and borderline subnormality, it seems unlikely that the causal factors, whether they are social or genetic, would apply to only one child in the family. We have, therefore, extended our analysis to the siblings of minimally subnormal children and have compared them with the siblings of children who are not mentally subnormal. Moreover, since social conditions of life would be expected to influence intellectual competence, whether or not any member of a sibship is mentally subnormal, the same factors have been applied to the entire population of children.

Family Characteristics of Minimally and Borderline Subnormal Children

Size of Family. In a comprehensive review of the literature, Anastasi (1956) presents evidence to suggest that there is a greater tendency for children in large families to have low intelligence test scores than for those in small families. We would, therefore, expect a higher proportion of minimally and borderline subnormal children to come from large families. As may be seen in Table 1, minimally subnormal children come from families having five children or more 2½ times as frequently as do the children in the comparison population. Borderline subnormal children come from large families twice as frequently as children in the comparison sample.

Area of Residence. In Aberdeen, 40 percent of families and 49 percent of individual persons live in houses and flats owned by the local authority, and certain areas of the city consist entirely of such housing facilities. Most of these "council houses" and tenements were built after 1945, but some of the tenements were built during the interwar period

TABLE 1.

Proportion of minimally subnormal, borderline subnormal, and comparison sample children living in families in Social Classes IV and V with various defined family characteristics

Family Characteristics	No. and Percentage of Children					
	Minimally subnormal		Borderline subnormal		Comparison sample	
	No.*	Percent	No.*	Percent	No.*	Percent
≧5 children	19 (30)	63†	24 (52)	46	9 (36)	25
Residence in interwar tenement	13 (30)	43†	12 (52)	23	6 (38)	16
Person/room ratio ≧2	16 (22)	73†	Information unavailable		12 (38)	32
Mother's premarital occupation: semi- or unskilled manual	22 (30)	73†	27 (46)	59	18 (37)	49

* Figures in parentheses represent the number of cases in each population for which information was available.

† The difference in proportions between the minimally subnormal and the comparison sample is significant at p < 0.05 using a one-tailed test.

to house families who had lived in the central area slums. Although few of the original slum dwellers currently reside in these tenements, a process of selection, mainly of choice but partly by administrative decision, persisted for many years by which a population socially similar to the original one still resides in these tenements. By administrative decision, frequently of a rather informal nature, "bad" tenants—those who are often late in paying rent or ones said to pay little attention to the state of repair and cleanliness of the house—were located in these interwar tenements. The stigma attached to these areas has also prompted socially aspiring families to request more "desirable" housing. Thus, these tenements contain a high proportion of unskilled and semi-skilled workers—many of whom are frequently unemployed—and "problem" families.

Table 1 shows that residence in interwar tenements occurs almost three times as frequently in the minimal subnormality group as in the comparison sample. There is no significant difference between the borderline and comparison groups.

Degree of Crowding. Information was available for the mentally subnormal and comparison groups on the number of rooms occupied by the family and the number of persons living in them. The number of rooms per house does not vary greatly in working class housing in Aberdeen, especially in the interwar tenements. While crowding is clearly a class-related variable, possibly useful in identifying high-risk groups, variations in levels of crowding are heavily affected by one of the variables already discussed, namely, size of family.

Table 1 shows that the proportion of families living in overcrowded conditions (two persons or more per room) is twice as high in the minimally subnormal group as in the comparison group.

Mother's Premarital Occupation. The mother's own occupation, indicative of her education, skill, and work milieu, provides a further measurement of the social position of the family. The tendency of people to marry a spouse with similar background and interests means, of course, that there is a close relationship between social class based on the father's occupation and that based on the mother's occupation, but there is sufficient variation for one measure to add further information to the other. Women's occupations after marriage are much affected by family responsibilities, so we have chosen premarital occupation as the better criterion of skill, education, and status.

Table 1 shows that the percentage of mothers who had semi- or unskilled manual jobs was 1½ times greater in the minimally subnormal sample than in the comparison group. The borderline group also had a higher proportion of such mothers than the comparison group, but the difference was not so great.

Combined Family Characteristics. Since the family characteristics which we have examined separately are present in various combinations in all families, we can determine whether, by examining combined characteristics, greater precision can be obtained in identifying those families in the lowest social classes that are at risk of having a minimally subnormal child. We shall restrict our analysis to Social Class V in order to test power of discrimination within a single occupational class. Since this class constraint reduces the number of cases for study, we have maintained a reasonable sample size by including all children administratively defined as mentally subnormal with an IQ of 50 or greater and without clinical evidence of central nervous system damage.

The two family characteristics selected for combined analysis are the number of children and the area of residence. These variables were selected both because relevant data were available for the total population of children under study and because they were the two variables in which the families of the minimally subnormal children differed most strongly from those in the total population.

On page 71, we showed that the prevalence rate of minimal subnormality in Social Class V as a whole is 18.1 per 1000. Table 2 shows that each of the family characteristics results in doubling of the rate over the general prevalence for Social Class V. When both characteristics are used jointly to identify families, a six-fold increase is obtained in the prevalence rate for minimal subnormality in Social Class V compared with the overall prevalence of Social Class V. Thus, the analysis of these two family characteristics in combination within Social Class

TABLE 2.

*Prevalence of minimal subnormality in Social Class V by family size and area of residence**

Family Characteristics	No. of Children Minimally Subnormal	No. of Children in Population at Risk	Prevalence per 1000
≧5 children..........................	13	336	38.7
Residence in interwar tenement..........	10	234	42.7
≧5 children and residence in interwar tenement................................	9	88	102.3

* In Social Class V, there are 18 cases of minimal subnormality, 1044 children in the population at risk, and a prevalence rate of 17.2 per 1000.

V enables us to identify with greater precision one set of families in which minimal subnormality is more likely to occur.†

Siblings of Minimally Subnormal Children. The factors which contribute to the causes of minimal subnormality in Social Classes IV and V may act uniquely on the child in the family who is minimally subnormal. This condition could occur, for example, if the child had been damaged from biologic causes which acted solely upon himself. If this were so, we would not expect the intellectual functioning of the siblings to be any different from that of the siblings of children in the comparison population.

Alternatively, the factors which contribute to minimal subnormality in the study children may also have an effect on their siblings. This effect might lead to mental subnormality or to varying degrees of intellectual impairment without mental subnormality.

The only way to determine the intellectual status of all siblings would be to wait until the families which we are studying had finished childbearing and all of the children were old enough to be given a definitive assessment of intellectual functioning. To prevent such a long delay, we have included only the siblings who had taken the Moray House Intelligence Test at age 7 by the date that this analysis was begun (1966). Because of the relationship between size of family and mental subnormality, we shall use as a control the number of siblings for whom intelligence test scores were available.

The clearest evidence of difference between the two groups of siblings is in their administrative designation as mentally subnormal and their placement in special schools. As may be noted in Table 3, the percentage of mentally subnormal siblings of minimally subnormal children is 12 times greater than that of the comparison population.

Table 4 shows that a higher proportion of the siblings of minimally subnormal children than of the comparison population who are in regular schools have intelligence test scores of less than 90. (Similar differences are found when a score of less than 80 is used.) Moreover, as shown in Table 5, a smaller proportion of siblings of minimally subnormal children than of siblings of the comparison population have high intelligence test scores. These findings strongly suggest that the familial factors associated with minimal subnormality are associated with reduced IQ in other children in the family as well.

---

† Only three minimally subnormal children in Social Class IV lived in interwar tenements. For this reason, when the same combined analysis was performed for Social Classes IV and V, family size and area of residence, when combined, gave a prevalence rate only slightly higher than family size or area of residence separately.

TABLE 3.

Proportion of mentally subnormal siblings of minimally subnormal children and of the comparison sample in Social Classes IV and V

No. of Siblings in Family*	No. and Percentage of Children			
	Siblings of mentally subnormal children		Siblings of comparative population	
	No.†	Percent	No.†	Percent
1	0 (5)	—	0 (13)	—
2	2 (14)	14.3	1 (18)	6.0
3	0 (15)	—	0 (33)	—
4	6 (16)	38.0	0 (16)	—
5	1 (10)	10.0	0 (10)	—
6	1 (18)	6.0	—	—
Total	10 (78)	12.8	1 (90)	1.1

* For whom intelligence tests were available.

† Figures in parentheses represent the number of cases in each population for which information was available.

TABLE 4.

Proportion of siblings of minimally subnormal children and of the comparison sample who are in regular schools and whose 7+ test scores are <90

No. of Siblings in Family*	No. and Percentage of Children			
	Siblings of mentally subnormal children		Siblings of comparative population	
	No.†	Percent	No.†	Percent
1	3 (5)	60	2 (13)	15
2	8 (14)	57	5 (18)	28
3	11 (15)	73	13 (33)	39
4	9 (16)	56	6 (16)	38
5	7 (10)	70	6 (10)	60
6	11 (18)	61	—	—
Total	49 (78)	63	32 (90)	36

* For whom intelligence tests were available.

† Figures in parentheses represent the number of cases in each population for which information was available.

We have thus been able to identify certain family conditions in Social Classes IV and V that are associated with higher and lower risks for the presence of minimal subnormality and low intelligence test scores. These conditions may be summarized as follows:

Higher risk	Lower risk
Five children or more	Fewer than five children
Residence in interwar tenement	Residence in other than interwar tenement
Person per room ratio of 2 or more	Person per room ratio of less than 2
Mother's premarital occupation: semi- or unskilled manual	Mother's premarital occupation: professional, clerical, or skilled.

From these findings, we would expect that the siblings of minimally subnormal children living in higher risk conditions would be more likely than the siblings of those living in lower risk conditions to be mentally subnormal or to perform at lower levels on intelligence tests. To examine this possibility, we have classified the families of the minimally subnormal children according to each of the higher and lower risk conditions and have calculated the percentage of mentally subnormal siblings and siblings with IQ scores of less than 80 at age 7. In addition to the family characteristics considered earlier, we have included poverty and family disorganization, each of which was rated on a three-point scale by raters who were without knowledge of the intelligence levels of siblings. Poverty was assessed by the amount of assistance given to the families by social and welfare agencies, and family disorganization was evaluated by such factors as prolonged unemployment, desertion by either or both parents, prison sentences, and evidence of neglect of the child. Clearly, the ratings of poverty and

TABLE 5.

Proportion of siblings of minimally subnormal children and of the comparison sample who are in regular schools and whose 7+ test scores are ≧100

No. of Siblings in Family*	No. and Percentage of Children			
	Siblings of mentally subnormal children		Siblings of comparative population	
	No.†	Percent	No.†	Percent
1	1 (5)	20	7 (13)	54
2	1 (14)	7	8 (18)	44
3	2 (15)	13	11 (33)	33
4	0 (16)	—	5 (16)	31
5	1 (10)	10	1 (10)	10
6	3 (18)	17	—	—
Total	8 (78)	10.3	32 (90)	35.6

* For whom intelligence tests were available.

† Figures in parentheses represent the number of cases in each population for which information was available.

TABLE 6.

Proportion of mentally subnormal siblings and siblings with IQ <80 by higher and lower risk conditions in current Social Classes IV and V

Family Characteristics	No. and Percentage of Children					
	Siblings who are mentally subnormal		Regular school siblings, IQ <80		Total of siblings in both groups	
	No.†	Percent	No.†	Percent	No.†	Percent
No. of children						
1–4	1 (18)	5.6	4 (18)	22	5 (18)	27.6
≧5	9 (60)	15	21 (60)	35	30 (60)	50
Area of residence						
Other housing	2 (40)	5	15 (40)	37.5	17 (40)	42.5
Interwar tenement	8 (38)	21	10 (38)	26	18 (38)	47
Person/room ratio*						
<2	0 (10)	—	2 (10)	20	2 (10)	20
≧2	5 (32)	16	12 (32)	37	17 (32)	53
Mother's premarital occupation						
More skilled	3 (23)	13	3 (23)	13	6 (23)	26
Semi- or unskilled manual	7 (55)	12.7	22 (55)	40	29 (55)	52.7
Family disorganization						
Slight or moderate	3 (41)	7	10 (41)	24	13 (41)	31
Severe	7 (37)	19	15 (37)	40	22 (37)	59
Poverty						
Slight or moderate	0 (16)	—	4 (16)	29	4 (16)	29
Severe	10 (62)	16	21 (62)	34	31 (62)	50

* There were 36 cases with no data.

† Figures in parentheses represent the number of cases in each population for which information was available.

family disorganization, like the other variables already considered, overlap to some degree.

The results are summarized in Table 6. For each characteristic we found a higher proportion of mentally subnormal siblings in the higher risk group than in the lower risk condition. Except for residence in interwar tenements, the proportion of siblings with low IQ scores is greater for higher risk conditions than for lower risk conditions. When the siblings who are mentally subnormal are combined with the siblings in regular schools who have an IQ of less than 80,‡ all of the results are

‡ Although all of the siblings being considered have taken the Moray House Intelligence Test at age 7, some of those with scores low enough to justify administrative designation as mentally subnormal might not as yet have been so designated. The most valid procedure for the purpose of this analysis, therefore, is to combine the two groups of siblings.

in the expected direction. This result provides further evidence that the factors contributing to mental subnormality in these higher risk families not only act on the minimally subnormal child but also have some influence on the sibling.

Family Characteristics and Intellectual Level of all 8- to 10-Year-Old Children who are not Mentally Subnormal

So far, our consideration of siblings has been restricted to families with a minimally subnormal child. If the high-risk conditions examined above, or more probably the environmental experiences to which they are related, have any etiologic significance, we would also expect them to be associated with poor intellectual functioning in other families in which they occur. To examine this possibility, we shall take the total population of children in Social Classes IV and V aged 8 to 10 who have an intelligence test performance of 80 or greater. All of these children are in regular schools and cannot, on psychometric grounds, be considered as mentally subnormal. For this population we shall determine for each family characteristic whether those children living in family conditions shown to be associated with greater risk of minimal mental subnormality have lower intelligence than do those children living in family conditions shown to be associated with lesser risk of mental subnormality. For each of these classifications we have calculated the percentage of children who, at age 7, have a Moray House Intelligence Test score of under 100.§

Table 7 shows that the proportion of children with low scores is lowest when there are one or two children in the family and increases steadily as the number of children increases.

Another high risk variable was housing. The greatest proportion of children with scores of less than 100 was found among those who live in the interwar tenements and the lowest proportion, in the housing areas consisting mainly of private homes (Table 8).

Although the association between the mother's premarital occupation and the children's intelligence (Table 9) is less clear-cut, the trend is in the expected direction—that is, a greater proportion of children with low scores have mothers whose premarital occupation required less skill and training.

For all of the family characteristics considered, our findings show that higher risk conditions are associated with lower levels of intelligence and suggest, therefore, that the factors which are associated with minimal subnormality in Social Classes IV and V also have a general

---

§ This score is closest to the median for this population of children.

TABLE 7.

Proportion of children 8 to 10 years old in Social Classes IV and V with IQ of 80 to 99 by size of family

No. of Children in Family	No. and Percentage of Children Scoring <100	
	No.*	Percent
1	33 (117)	28.2
2	116 (403)	28.8
3	176 (463)	38.0
4	171 (375)	45.6
5	134 (260)	51.5
6	77 (130)	59.2
≧7	58 (110)	52.7

* Figures in parentheses represent the number of cases in each population for which information was available.

TABLE 8.

Proportion of children 8 to 10 years old in Social Classes IV and V with IQ of 80 to 99 by area of residence

Area of Residence	No. and Percentage of Children Scoring <100	
	No.*	Percent
Mainly private housing......................	120 (358)	33.5
Council housing............................	456 (1175)	38.8
Interwar tenement..........................	187 (321)	58.3

* Figures in parentheses represent the number of cases in each population for which information was available.

association with levels of intellectual competence in the total population of children within these social classes.

Summary and Discussion

Our consideration of the families of the minimally subnormal children within Social Classes IV and V has resulted in the following findings:

1. Minimal subnormality is overrepresented in families characterized by a size of five children or more, residence in interwar tenements, crowded housing conditions, and mothers who were engaged in semi- and unskilled manual occupations prior to marriage;

TABLE 9.

Proportion of children 8 to 10 years old in Social Classes IV and V with IQ of 80 to 99 by mother's premarital occupation

Mother's Premarital Occupation	No. and Percentage of Children Scoring <100	
	No.*	Percent
Professional or technical...............	4 (8)	50
Clerical................................	21 (109)	19.3
Distributive...........................	87 (221)	39.4
Skilled manual.........................	155 (411)	37.7
Semiskilled manual.....................	162 (370)	43.8
Unskilled manual.......................	71 (149)	47.7
Fishworker.............................	162 (319)	50.8

* Figures in parentheses represent the number of cases in each population for which information was available.

2. Borderline subnormality is overrepresented in the same types of family though not to the same extent as minimal subnormality;

3. When, within Social Class V, the family characteristics of five children or more and residence in interwar tenements are analyzed together, greater precision is achieved in identifying families at risk of having an 8- to 10-year-old minimally subnormal child than when each characteristic is examined separately;

4. There is an association between higher risk conditions and lower intellectual functioning among the siblings of minimally subnormal children in Social Classes IV and V;

5. The association between higher risk conditions and lower intellectual functioning exists in the population of all 8- to 10-year-old children in Social Classes IV and V who are not mentally subnormal.

We would like to examine other clinical subtypes of mental subnormality in order to determine whether the conditions of risk for other clinical subtypes of mental subnormality are influenced by family characteristics. Unfortunately, for these other subtypes, there is insufficient homogeneity of social class to provide a sufficient number of cases for analysis.

The use of an array of class-related variables has enabled us, even within a restricted occupational class, to identify conditions in which the prevalence of minimal mental subnormality is substantially higher than that of the class as a whole. By the simultaneous use of sibling data, we have been able to establish that the high risk applies to other children in the family and not only to the mentally subnormal child who provided the starting point of our inquiry. Our indicators, therefore, powerfully define high and low risk. But are they any more than that? Do they provide clues to a possible etiology for minimal subnormality?

The association between our indicators and minimal and borderline subnormality, strong though it may be, provides no definitive evidence for separating out the relative contributions of social and genetic factors or their interaction. Every "social fact" presented in this chapter could be used to support a genetic explanation. It is also possible that more sensitive measures or additional data might reveal evidence of biologic defect in the child which we have been unable to detect. In the following chapters we shall examine one set of biologic factors, namely, obstetric and perinatal complications, which may contribute to defect in the child. Nevertheless, the strength of the associations between social variables and minimal subnormality gives good cause for speculating about the possible ways in which the social experience of these children might have contributed to subnormality. Against this background, it is profitable to look at the possible causal meanings of class-related indicators.

Ideally we would like to observe, codify, and analyze variations in normative systems, particularly those concerned explicitly with child socialization. This goal is difficult to accomplish for large populations or samples. Such class-related variables as we have used are relatively easy to obtain. Unfortunately, they only lead us to the search area without specifying that aspect of the child's interaction with his environment for which we search. In the following discussion, therefore, we can only speculate about possible etiologic interpretations.

The strong association between subnormality and family size may be interpreted in several ways, either singly or in combination. The first interpretation postulates a genetic mechanism by which parents of low intelligence have large families and transmit their low intelligence to their numerous offspring. While our data are not appropriate for the further exploration of this hypothesis, we recognize that they are consistent with a genetic interpretation. An environmental explanation, which has carried more weight in recent years, is summarized by Hunt (p. 343, 1961) as follows:

A preponderant portion of the evidence appears to favor the hypothesis that the negative correlations between number of siblings and intelligence derives from the fact that children in larger families, especially those in which children are closely spaced, tend to get less adult care and varied stimulation during the early months than is got by children in smaller families, and especially those in which children are widely spaced.

The total picture presented by our interviewers' material leads us to advance a further and somewhat different hypothesis. In this hypothesis the emphasis is placed more upon the type of parents who have large families than upon the direct effect of "sibling density." Such parents, in a largely Protestant community, where family planning is practicable and is, in fact, practiced by a sizable section of the population, tend to be relatively fatalistic, to have low aspirations, to feel unable or unwilling to exercise control over their lives and their environment, and to be present- rather than future-oriented. These characteristics, manifest in the parents' apparent inability to plan their family growth, imply a set of value orientations which are incompatible with academic success. They indicate the existence of a subculture rooted in that economic insecurity which hitherto has been inseparable from the less skilled manual occupations. In such family milieux, attitudes toward education and academic achievement are indifferent, if not hostile, and the school may be perceived by the children as an alien environment, representing alien values.

Residence in the interwar tenements carries rather similar connotations. Areas of cities, even particular streets and blocks, acquire over their history a certain reputation, good or bad. In a situation where the town places almost one-half of its population in municipally owned and rent-controlled houses, and where exchange between tenants is allowed, some degree of social segregation becomes inevitable. In this way the socially mobile become residentially mobile, while those who have perhaps neither the aspiration nor the fully paid-up rent book remain in the least desirable areas. Since 90 percent of the flats in these areas have four habitable rooms or fewer, and since families in the high-risk group tend to be large, overcrowding is frequently a problem. Thus, residence in the interwar tenements carries many possible meanings—low social aspirations, low or uncertain income, poor domestic financial management, physical overcrowding, and the cultural level of a socially and educationally segregated community—none of which provides a favorable setting for the socialization of the child into an educationally oriented society.

Earlier research on occupational class in Aberdeen demonstrated that, within classes defined by the father's occupation, the premarital occupation of the mother correlates highly with area of residence, premarital conception, and the IQ scores of the children. Indeed, male occupation groups may be ranked for social status according to the proportion of the group marrying semiskilled or unskilled wives (Oldman & Illsley, 1966). The very high percentage of minimally subnormal and borderline children in Social Classes IV and V with semiskilled or unskilled mothers, compared with the general population, signifies that we are here dealing with the lowest status groups in the community.

Social Class V, in the Registrar-General's Classification of Occupations, contains not only casual laborers but also, for example, dockers, whose work is not devoid of skill and whose pay compares favorably with that in more skilled occupations. Duration of unemployment and, particularly, a high rate of long-term unemployment suggest that a considerable proportion of the fathers of mentally subnormal children are casual laborers rather than workers in the more stable, secure occupations.

Our argument would suggest, therefore, that a number of family characteristics distinguish the minimally and borderline subnormal children from other families in Social Classes IV and V. These characteristics are highly interrelated and, taken together, they identify those groups of the population with low status and aspirations, minimal education, poverty, family disorganization, and unwillingness or inability to plan the major economic and marital aspects of their lives. Such characteristics serve to identify certain of the families of minimally subnormal children, but by no means all of them.

This, then, is the microenvironmental setting associated with the highest prevalence of minimally and borderline subnormal children. We must make it quite clear that we do not imply that low occupational class, large family size, overcrowding, or slum living *causes* mental subnormality. The statement by Kohn (1963) which we applied to father's social class in the previous chapter applies equally well to the present problem:

> ... the intricate interplay of all these variables creates different basic conditions of life at different levels of the social order. Members of different social classes, by virtue of enjoying (or suffering) different conditions of life, come to see the world differently—to develop different conceptions of social reality, different aspirations and hopes and fears, different conceptions of the desirable.

While clearly, social environment must exercise a strong influence on the motivations, achievement, and development of the child, we cannot, on the basis of the present study, answer the crucial question as to how these background factors are translated into levels of ability or how they interact with other biologic or genetic influences.

Clearly, a fuller understanding of cause requires a conjoined consideration of both biologic and social-environmental conditions of risk. One important aspect of this interaction, the relationship between social class and obstetric events, is more fully considered in the next two chapters.

8

Pregnancy, Birth, and Perinatal Status in Mentally Subnormal Children and in the Population as a Whole

In the present chapter we continue our analysis of potential causal mechanisms in mental subnormality by considering the relations between subtypes of that dysfunction and features of pregnancy, birth, and perinatal status. Despite some contradictory findings, earlier investigations (reviewed by MacMahon & Sowa, 1961; Masland *et al*, 1958; Montague, 1962; Pasamanick & Knobloch, 1966) leave little doubt that there are general statistical associations between abnormalities in obstetric and perinatal condition and defective intellectual outcome. Since the reviews of the earlier research have been exceptionally complete, it is unnecessary for us to survey once again the wide range of literature. However, selected studies will be considered in relation to specific analyses.

Investigations conducted in the past frequently have lacked systematic obstetric detail, have had few specific measures of the clinical status of the mentally subnormal children, and have been carried out on small or biased populations. (For an analysis of major methodologic problems, see, for example, the reviews by Grimm and by Illsley, 1967.) It has been difficult to determine whether the associations obtained between obstetric and perinatal events and mental subnormality have reflected true linkages or whether they are adventitious products deriving from the study of socially and clinically biased samples in which obstetric complications and defective intellectual outcomes were both highly prevalent. In the present study, some of these limitations have been minimized because of the nature of the sample and because systematic, uniform, accurate, and relatively comprehensive obstetric

91

and perinatal information was available for almost all Aberdeen births, as was basic social and demographic information on the families in which the births occurred. Since the records from which such data have been drawn were not compiled specifically for the purpose of studying mental subnormality, certain biochemical and neurologic information obtained in infancy, as well as genetic and familial information, which would have been most useful for this purpose, was not available. Even with these limitations, however, the available data make it possible to identify the presence or absence of major disturbances of pregnancy, delivery, and newborn condition and to relate these factors to specific measures of intellectual functioning and neurologic status in the mentally subnormal children whom we have studied at school age.

It is easy to underestimate the complexity of the relation of obstetric and perinatal complications to mental subnormality and mistakenly to interpret their higher frequency of occurrence in subnormal samples, as compared with that in the population at large, as direct evidence for causation. However, as we already know from the data presented in earlier chapters, the mentally subnormal population as a whole is over-represented in large families of low socio-economic status. Some of the obstetric factors presumed to be relevant, such as low birth weight and bleeding, occur more frequently in the lower social classes and it is possible that their statistical association with mental subnormality merely reflects the different social prevalence of these complications rather than a causal link. Moreover, many obstetric complications are related to parity, and the overrepresentation of larger families in the mentally subnormal group suggests that higher pregnancy number may underlie the frequency with which certain complications are noted. Consequently, without appropriate controls for social class and pregnancy number, it is not possible to determine whether obstetric and perinatal complications truly are excessively frequent in the birth histories of mentally subnormal children. Since, in our study, data were available for the whole population, clinically and socially defined sub-groupings of mentally subnormal children could be compared with unaffected children in the relevant segments of the population from which they derived.

At another level, interpretation is made difficult by the fact that the mentally subnormal population is heterogeneous with respect both to the degree of intellectual deficit and to the degree to which mental subnormality is accompanied by the presence or absence of clinical signs of central nervous system damage. Clearly, analyses of total populations of mentally subnormal children and comparisons of their obstetric backgrounds with those of the general population have value. However, there is abundant evidence (Penrose, 1963; Masland *et al*, 1958; Ellis, 1963; Stevens & Heber, 1964) proving that different subtypes of mentally subnormal children differ markedly in the degree to which they exhibit direct or indirect manifestations of biologic defect. Moreover, different subtypes among the mentally subnormal children also differ in social background characteristics (*cf*. Chapter 6). Therefore, the fusing of subtypes when analyzing the association of mental subnormality with obstetric and perinatal antecedents has the inherent risks of failing to identify significant linkages when they do exist and of falsely attributing the causal meaning of such associations to subvariants of the disorder in which such linkages may, in fact, be absent.

In the present study we have tried to take account of these difficulties by basing the analysis of the associations on our previous analysis of clinical characteristics. Moreover, since the different subtypes of mental subnormality have very different social class distributions (see Chapters 6 and 7), such differences also need to be considered in an examination of the obstetric and perinatal antecedents in mental subnormality. Thus, in this chapter and the succeeding chapter, our considerations will be concerned not merely with the general association of reproductive antecedents in the mentally subnormal group as a whole, but also with the degree to which such antecedents relate to types of mental subnormality and social subsegments of children with the disorder.

Constraints and Expectations

In the present chapter our consideration of the relation of mental subnormality, its subtypes and social context, to reproductive and perinatal complications will have a broadly epidemiologic focus. Our principal analyses will involve external comparisons between the mentally subnormal children and relevant subsegments of the comparison population. In the main, we shall consider separately each of the complications of obstetric course and perinatal condition and shall compare the relative frequency of their occurrence in the mentally subnormal children with their prevalence in the socially appropriate comparison population. In certain instances, where the complications are related to pregnancy number (*i.e.*, the number of pregnancies experienced by the woman, including the current pregnancy), the comparison population will also be standardized for this factor.

In undertaking analysis of obstetric and perinatal factors, it is necessary to bear in mind that perinatal complications frequently occur in combination; *e.g.*, there is sometimes the coincidence of twinning, preeclamptic toxemia, breech delivery, and low birth weight. It is, therefore, not sufficient to present data for each complication separately, since a high frequency of any given complication may be the reflection of its coincidence with other more important phenomena. Alternatively, damage may occur or may be intensified if disturbances are piled upon one another. Identification of obstetric and perinatal risk, rather than the mere recognition of the presence of an abnormal circumstance, requires intensive clinical case study and evaluation. In the next chapter, therefore, we shall consider the effects of the major complications in combination as well as separately and shall engage in a more detailed consideration of particular pregnancies and families as well as of the joint influence of social and obstetric factors, which may help to clarify some issues.

The analysis of obstetric and perinatal factors will be restricted to a consideration of 92 of the 104 mentally subnormal children who have been intensively studied. Excluded from consideration are all children not born in Aberdeen; all children with Down's Syndrome (mongolism), in connection with which a chromosomal rather than an obstetric etiology is clearly present; and the one child in whom a cause for mental subnormality (encephalitis) was known to be present in later childhood.

Prior studies provide a basis for anticipating the differential frequency with which obstetric and perinatal complications will be found among the subtypes. Clearly, the greatest likelihood of finding excessive obstetric and perinatal complications would be expected for that clinical subtype of mental subnormality in which IQ is less than 50 and in which central nervous system damage is evident on clinical examination. Conversely, we would least strongly expect to find obstetric and perinatal complications in children with IQs of 60 or higher and with no evidence of central nervous system damage.

We already know that the minimally subnormal children as a whole are overrepresented in the lower social classes, whereas severely subnormal children are randomly distributed across social classes. Therefore, in all instances in which subtypes are compared with the reference population for prevalence of perinatal complications, comparison will involve social class constraints appropriate to the social composition of the subtype being considered.

There are insufficient cases of mental subnormality in the population and age range that we have studied to control completely and simultaneously for all variables of both social class and parity. However, this limitation may, in part, be overcome by first determining whether each obstetric and perinatal factor is related to social class and/or parity and then, when such associations are found and numbers are adequate, by introducing pregnancy number as a further control.

The analysis to be presented is concerned with three sets of obstetric and perinatal events—complications of pregnancy, complications of labor and delivery, and the child's characteristics as a newborn infant. In addition, because the mother's biologic characteristics, such as her age and height, even in the absence of identifiable complications of pregnancy, may exert an important indirect influence on the child's development *in utero*, these factors will be considered as well. Where the number of cases makes it possible, statistical tests have been applied. In other instances, because of small numbers, only directional trends have been noted.

Complications of Pregnancy

Pregnancy may be complicated by the presence of a host of conditions which are potentially damaging to the fetus and are capable of producing consequences ranging from death, at one extreme, to normal outcomes, at the other. Pasamanick and Lilienfeld (1955), in viewing this range of consequences associated with pre- and perinatal complications, have advanced the concept of a "continuum of reproductive casualty" to embrace the phenomena. In the present study we are considering only one type of defective outcome, mental subnormality, and are analyzing the degree to which it may be viewed as a "reproductive casualty."

We shall start by dealing with three common complications of pregnancy which have received considerable attention in previous investigations as possible factors in the production of mental subnormality—preeclamptic toxemia, as reflected in blood pressure, albuminuria, and edema; threatened abortion, as indicated by bleeding before the 29th week; and antepartum hemorrhage, as indicated by bleeding after this date. Since various definitions of these conditions have contributed to contrary findings in reports from different centers, their definitions as used in Aberdeen are presented in Appendix 5. The relative frequencies with which each of these complications occurred in the mentally subnormal and comparison groups are given in Figure 1.

The frequency of all grades of preeclamptic toxemia and hypertensive disease was not very different in the mentally subnormal and comparison groups (20.6 and 16.7 percent, respectively). This lack of difference was entirely attributable to cases of mild preeclampsia, characterized largely by some hypertension, which were slightly more

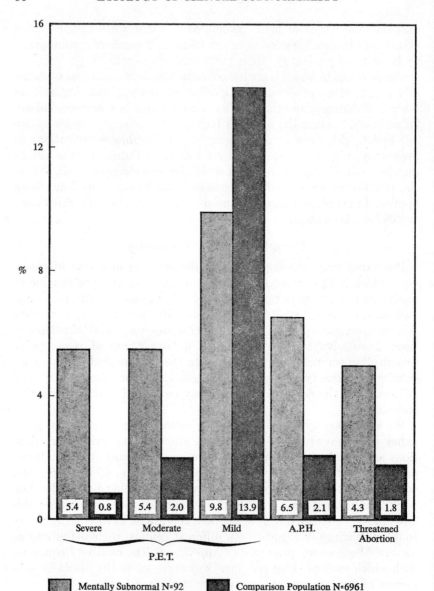

Figure 1. Distribution of three complications of pregnancy in the mothers of the mentally subnormal and comparison populations. P.E.T., preeclamptic toxemia; A.P.H., antepartum hemorrhage.

prevalent in the comparison population of mothers. However, both severe and moderate preeclampsia were present with significantly greater frequency in the mothers of the mentally subnormal children. The difference between the two groups was most striking for severe preeclampsia, which occurred six times more often in the mothers of the mentally subnormal children than in the comparison population. Moderate preeclampsia was less strikingly overrepresented but still appeared almost three times more frequently in the mothers of the mentally subnormal group than in the comparison population.

Bleeding, manifested both as antepartum hemorrhage and as threatened abortion, was noted significantly more frequently in the pregnancies resulting in mentally subnormal children. Threatened abortions were twice as frequent and antepartum hemorrhage was present three times as frequently in the mothers of the mentally subnormal children as in the comparison group. The overall prevalence of bleeding of both types during pregnancy was thus approximately three times as great in the pregnancies resulting in the mentally subnormal group as in the comparison population of children.

The frequencies of these complications varied by social class and by pregnancy number. Thus, all categories of preeclampsia, particularly the severe and moderate types, tended in general to be more common in earlier than in later pregnancies and in the upper social grouping. In contrast, both forms of bleeding occurred more frequently in the young multiparae and the older grand multiparae, types of women who are most commonly found in the lower social strata. It was possible, therefore, that the differences in prevalence that we have noted reflect a population of mothers which, because of its composition by social class and parity, was highly at risk for these complications and that these differences are not necessarily an indication of the uniquely damaging effects of pregnancy complications on the fetus. However, since the mentally subnormal group as a whole is overrepresented for higher parity and lower social class groups in which toxemia is not excessively present, our finding for this disorder may well be an underestimation. The obverse of this line of reasoning may hold for bleeding.

For the reasons which have just been advanced, the frequency with which preeclampsia occurred in the different subtypes of mental subnormality was compared with the frequency of these events in segments of the general population which were comparable for both social class and pregnancy number (Table 1). Viewed as a whole, these data indicate that severe toxemia tended to be more frequently present in the cases with IQs below 60, whether or not central nervous system damage

TABLE 1.

Frequency of occurrence of preeclamptic toxemia in the mothers of the mentally subnormal and comparison populations, matched for social class and pregnancy number

Subtype*	No. of Cases of Preeclamptic Toxemia								
	Severe			Moderate			Mild		
	Ob-served	Ex-pected	O/E†	Ob-served	Ex-pected	O/E†	Ob-served	Ex-pected	O/E†
<50; CNS+ (20)	2	0.31	6.5	0	0.59	0	3	3.48	0.9
≥50; CNS+ (24)	2	0.18	11.1	3	0.36	8.3	1	2.64	0.4
50–59; CNS− (10)	1	0.08	12.5	0	0.19	0	1	1.13	0.1
≥60; CNS− (37)	0	0.19	0	1	0.55	1.8	2	3.59	0.6

* Defined by IQ and presence of central nervous system damage. Figures in parentheses represent the number of cases in each population for which information was available.

† Cases observed/cases expected.

was present. However, an acceptable level of statistical significance is reached only for the CNS+ cases. A moderate degree of preeclamptic toxemia was present significantly more frequently in the subtype characterized by an IQ of 50 or greater and by associated clinical findings of neurologic damage. No excess of mild preeclampsia was found for any of the subtypes.

Both antepartum hemorrhage and threatened abortion as reflected in bleeding were more frequent in each of the subtypes than in the standardized populations with which they were compared. However, given the rate in the general population, the absolute number of cases was too small for statistical significance to be achieved in any of the subtypes. It is of interest to note that the mothers of children in the most severely affected subtype experienced bleeding with a frequency almost equivalent to that found in the general population. In contrast, children in all other subtypes derived from pregnancies in which bleeding was three times as frequent as was the case for normal pregnancies (Table 2).

Considered as a whole, our data suggest that both preeclamptic toxemia and bleeding were more frequent in pregnancies which resulted in mentally subnormal children. Preeclamptic toxemia was overrepresented in the subtype having both severity of intellectual handicap and clinical evidence of central nervous system damage, whereas bleed-

TABLE 2.

Frequency of both antepartum hemorrhage and threatened abortion in the mothers of the mentally subnormal and comparison populations, matched for social class and pregnancy number

Subtype*	No. of Cases of Antepartum Hemorrhage and Threatened Abortion		
	Observed	Expected	O/E†
<50; CNS+ (20)	1	0.78	1.3
≧50; CNS+ (24)	3	0.94	3.2
50–59; CNS− (10)	2	0.45	4.4
≧60; CNS− (36)	4	1.41	2.8

* Defined by IQ and presence of central nervous system damage. Figures in parentheses represent the number of cases in each population for which information was available.

† Cases observed/cases expected.

ing was overrepresented in the subtypes having milder degrees of impairment. It should be remembered, however, that such associations do not necessarily imply causation. Preeclamptic toxemia, apart from its greatest frequency in first and second pregnancies, is also associated with poor fetal growth and prematurity and is particularly common in multiple births. This topic and other questions relevant to the etiologic role of the individual pregnancy complications will be evaluated from a clinical obstetric standpoint in the next chapter.

Duration of Labor

Abnormalities of labor, reflected either in its length or in its relation to type of delivery, may affect the likelihood of injury to the child. Nesbitt (1957), in considering perinatal loss, has identified both very long and very short labors, among other conditions, with death and injury. Eastman (1956) also has argued that labor of long duration has attendant hazards of trauma, infection, anoxia, and asphyxia, all conditions which place the infant's nervous system at risk and have consequences of cerebral palsy and mental subnormality. Excessively short labor, too, has been implicated as contributing to these defective outcomes (Masland et al, 1958).

Although many types of complication may occur during labor, we shall reserve a consideration of most of these for the next chapter. In this chapter, we shall restrict our attention to a comparison of the duration of labor in the births resulting in the mentally subnormal and com-

TABLE 3.

Distribution of duration of labor in the births of children in the mentally subnormal and comparison populations

Duration of Labor (hours)	No. and Percentage of Children			
	Mentally subnormal		Comparison population	
	No.	Percent	No.	Percent
≦3	14	16.5	798	10.9
>3 and <24	64	75.3	5670	77.2
≧24	7	8.2	881	11.9

parison populations of children. The data presented in Table 3, except for some excess of labors of short duration, provide no evidence that the labors which resulted in mentally subnormal children were excessively short or long. With this exception, the lack of overall difference in the duration of labor in the two groups considered is clearly shown in the cumulative frequency percentage curve for the duration of labor (Figure 2). An analysis of duration of labor by social class in the mentally subnormal group suggests an overrepresentation of prolonged labor in the upper social class and a slight excess of short labors in all classes.

When the duration of labor in the subtypes of mental subnormality was considered (Table 4), no substantial differences were found to exist between duration of labor in the most severely handicapped children and in the general population. In this table, as in all subsequent ones, the most severe subtype is compared with the total comparison population since no social class gradient existed for this subtype. The least severely subnormal are compared only with Social Classes IV and V, because these classes were heavily overrepresented in this subtype. For cases of intermediate severity, the appropriate comparison value lies somewhere between the overall comparison value and that for Social Classes IV and V. This comparison is made because the subtypes of intermediate severity are slightly overrepresented in the lower social classes. Children with evidence of central nervous system damage but with IQs equal to or greater than 50, as well as those with no clinical evidence of central nervous system damage and with IQs between 50 and 59, were the products of labor of exceptionally short duration two and one-half times as frequently as were children in the same general

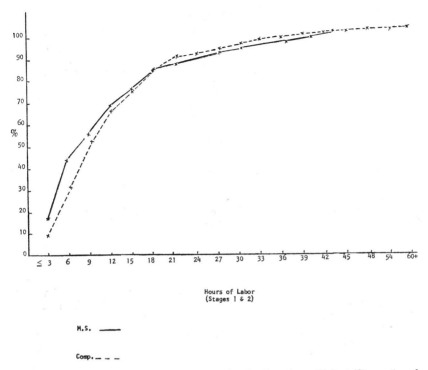

Hours of Labor
(Stages 1 & 2)

M.S.   ⎯⎯

Comp. ⎯ ⎯ ⎯

Figure 2. Cumulative percentage curves for the duration of labor (Stages 1 and 2) in the mentally subnormal and comparison groups.

population. Children with the mildest degrees of mental subnormality came from labors of short duration as frequently as was the case in the segment of the general population with which they are appropriately compared. It is of interest that prolonged labor was no more frequent and, in fact, tended to be slightly less prevalent in this clinical type of mental subnormality than in the comparison group. Pregnancy number did not contribute to these differences.

The analysis of length of labor did not suggest a general relation to mental subnormality. However, short labors were overrepresented in cases of intermediate severity. It was possible that labors of very short duration were associated with low birth weight, short gestation, and multiple births. The interrelation of social class, pregnancy number, and clinical events at labor are considered in detail in Chapter 9.

TABLE 4.

Relation of duration of labor to the births of children in the subtypes of mental subnormality

Subtype*	Duration of Labor (hours)	Percentage of Children	
		Mentally subnormal	Comparison population
<50; CNS+ (19)	≦3	5.3	10.9†
	≧24	15.8	11.9†
≧50; CNS+ (22)	≦3	27.3	
	≧24	4.5	
50–59; CNS− (8)	≦3	25.0	
	≧24	12.5	
≧60; CNS− (34)	≦3	14.7	11.97‡
	≧24	2.9	7.37‡

* Defined by IQ and presence of central nervous system damage. Figures in parentheses represent the number of cases in each population for which information was available.

† All social classes, 7349 cases.

‡ Social Classes IV and V, 2063 cases.

Complications of Presentation and Delivery

Among the abnormalities of presentation and delivery most frequently cited as potential causes for damage to the child are breech presentation and instrumental delivery. The prevalence of breech and other malpresentations was approximately two times as great in the mentally subnormal population (Table 5).

Another frequently cited cause of subnormality is multiple birth. Multiple births in the mentally subnormal group occurred twice as often as in the general population.

No differences were found in the frequency of spontaneous deliveries and in the use of forceps.

Cesarean section was less frequent in the mentally subnormal group than in the comparison population. Any association with cesarean section is necessarily indirect, since this operation is performed very frequently for complications of labor or fetal distress, factors which themselves may influence outcome. In the past, most sections were done for prolonged or obstructed labor; more recently, fetal indications have

TABLE 5.

Frequency of types of presentation and delivery in the mentally subnormal and comparison populations

Type of Presentation or Delivery	No. and Percentage of Children			
	Mentally subnormal		Comparison population	
	No.*	Percent	No.*	Percent
Spontaneous......................	80 (92)	86.9	6140 (6955)	88.3
Cesarean section.................	1 (92)	1.1	215 (6955)	3.1
Forceps.........................	6 (92)	6.5	453 (6955)	6.5
Breech or other malpresentation....	5 (92)	5.4	147 (6955)	2.1
Multiple births†	5 (92)	5.4	208 (6955)	2.9

* Figures in parentheses represent the number of cases in each population for which information was available.

† Number and percentage of multiple births are independent of type of delivery.

increasingly been used as a basis for decision. A cesarean section may also be done for indications which include maternal age, parity, and previous history of obstetric difficulties, as well as previous cesarean section. In these latter situations, the obstetrician elects to do a section before the onset of labor. Thus, the reason for the cesarean section may well be of greater importance in defining the condition of the baby than is the operation itself. This point will be considered further in the next chapter.

As may be seen in Table 6, complications of delivery were excessively present in the most severely mentally subnormal children. In this group, forceps, breech, and other malpresentations, as well as multiple births, were overrepresented. Breech and other malpresentations are overrepresented in all subtypes except that with IQ between 50 and 59 and no evidence of central nervous system damage. However, it is perhaps misleading to consider these complications singly since, in most instances, at least two of the conditions occurred together. Moreover, particular complications of delivery are related to maternal age and pregnancy number. These issues are considered in Chapter 9.

Condition of the Child as a Neonate

There are divergent and even conflicting opinions as to the relation

TABLE 6.

Relation of types of delivery to the subtypes of mental subnormality

Subtype*	Type of Presentation or Delivery	Percentage of Children	
		Mentally subnormal	Comparison population
<50; CNS+ (20)	Spontaneous	80.0	88.3†
	Cesarean section	—	3.1†
	Forceps	10.0	6.5†
	Breech or other malpresentation	10.0	2.1†
	Multiple births‡	10.0	2.9†
≧50; CNS+ (24)	Spontaneous	91.7	
	Cesarean section	—	
	Forceps	4.2	
	Breech or other malpresentation	4.2	
	Multiple births‡	4.2	
50–59; CNS− (10)	Spontaneous	100.0	
	Cesarean section	—	
	Forceps	—	
	Breech or other malpresentation	—	
	Multiple births‡	—	
≧60; CNS− (36)	Spontaneous	86.1	91.3§
	Cesarean section	2.8	2.0§
	Forceps	5.6	4.6§
	Breech or other malpresentation	5.6	2.1§
	Multiple births‡	2.8	2.5§

　　* Defined by IQ and presence of central nervous system damage. Figures in parentheses represent the number of cases in each population for which information was available.

　　† All social classes, 6955 cases.

　　‡ Percentage of multiple births is independent of type of delivery.

　　§ Social Classes IV and V, 2063 cases.

of neonatal status to mental subnormality. For three of the most important major indicators of neonatal status—birth weight, gestational age, and the condition of the infant at birth—one finds in one country, or even in one city, different opinions as to the importance of these factors as potential causes for mental subnormality. Drillien (1964) and Douglas (1960), both reporting from Edinburgh, although on different samples of children, differed in their assessment of the importance of prematurity, as judged by weight, in predisposing children to mental subnormality. Other studies, of which the reports of Fairweather and Illsley (1960), Knobloch and Pasamanick (1959), Graham *et al* (1957), and McDonald (1964) are representative, have either found or failed to find an association between subnormal intellectual functioning and such factors as low birth weight, asphyxia, cyanosis, and disturbance of muscle tone and function in the newborn.

Birth Weight. The distribution of birth weight for mentally subnormal and total populations of children are presented in Table 7. As may be noted from the table, children of low birth weight are markedly overrepresented in the mentally subnormal group. Thus, 33 percent of the mentally subnormal children, in contrast to 12 percent of the comparison population, weighed less than 6 pounds at birth. Clearly, low birth weight children were significantly overrepresented and higher birth weight children were significantly underrepresented in the mentally subnormal group.

When low birth weight, as estimated by a birth weight of less than 6 pounds, is considered by social class in the mentally subnormal and comparison populations (Table 8), it is seen that low birth weight is overrepresented for the mentally subnormal children in all social classes. The prevalance across the different social classes of infants who weighed less than 6 pounds was two to five times as great in the mentally subnormal as in the comparison population.

As may be seen from Table 9, low birth weight was overrepresented at all ranges of pregnancy number in the mentally subnormal population. The greatest degrees of overrepresentation occurred in first and

TABLE 7.

Distribution of birth weight in the mentally subnormal and comparison populations

Birth Weight (pounds)	No. and Percentage of Children			
	Mentally subnormal		Comparison population	
	No.	Percent	No.	Percent
≦3	4	4.3⎫	43	0.6⎫
>3–5	7	7.6⎬32.6	138	2.0⎬11.5
5–6	19	20.7⎭	617	8.9⎭
6–7	25	27.2	1910	27.5
7–8	23	25.0	2524	36.3
8–9	11	12.0	132	19.0
≧9	3	3.2	393	5.7
Total	92		6946	

TABLE 8.

Distribution of low birth weight (<6 pounds) by social class in the mentally subnormal and comparison populations

Social Class	No. and Percentage of Children			
	Mentally subnormal		Comparison population	
	No.*	Percent	No.*	Percent
I–IIIa	3 (6)	50.0	146 (1466)	10.0
IIIb, IIIc	11 (34)	32.4	335 (3080)	10.8
IV	2 (9)	22.2	124 (945)	13.1
V	14 (42)	33.3	148 (1114)	13.3

* Figures in parentheses represent the number of cases in each population for which information was available.

in second through fourth pregnancies, with low birth weight babies for these pregnancy numbers four and five times as frequent respectively as in the comparison group. These data appear to be independent of social class.

The relation of low birth weight to subtypes in the mentally subnormal sample is reflected in the data presented in Table 10. As may be seen from these data, the most severely handicapped children weighed less than 6 pounds at birth three times as frequently as the children in the comparison population. Low birth weight, too, was excessively present in those children with IQs of 50 or greater who had central nervous system damage—with almost four times as many such children as children in the comparison population weighing less than 6 pounds at birth. The least severely handicapped children did not exhibit the same

TABLE 9.

Relation of low birth weight (<6 pounds) to pregnancy number in the mentally subnormal and comparison populations

Pregnancy No.	Percentage of Children	
	Mentally subnormal	Comparison population
1	46.0	12.5
2–4	32.7	6.0
≧5	15.8	10.0

TABLE 10.

Relation of birth weight to the subtypes of mental subnormality and to the comparison population

Subtype*	Birth Weight (pounds)	Percentage of Children	
		Mentally subnormal	Comparison population
<50; CNS+ (22)	<4	5.0	0.6†
	4–5	5.0	2.0†
	5–6	25.0	9.0†
	6–7	25.0	27.0†
	7–8	25.0	36.4†
	8–9	10.0	19.0†
	≧9	5.0	6.0†
≧50; CNS+ (25)	<4	8.0	
	4–5	12.5	
	5–6	25.0	
	6–7	25.0	
	7–8	8.0	
	8–9	17.0	
	≧9	4.0	
50–59; CNS− (8)	<4	10.0	
	4–5	—	
	5–6	10.0	
	6–7	30.0	
	7–8	20.0	
	8–9	20.0	
	≧9	10.0	
≧60; CNS− (37)	<4	—	0.7‡
	4–5	8.0	2.0‡
	5–6	16.0	10.0‡
	6–7	30.0	28.8‡
	7–8	38.0	35.0‡
	8–9	8.0	17.3‡
	≧9	—	6.0‡

* Defined by IQ and presence of central nervous system damage. Figures in parentheses represent the number of cases in each population for which information was available.

† All social classes, 6946 cases.

‡ Social Classes IV and V, 2059 cases.

degree of overrepresentation of infants with low birth weight. However, even in this subtype, infants under 6 pounds were almost twice as frequent as in the relevant lower class comparison population.

Higher pregnancy number is most frequent in the lowest social classes. Low birth weight, however, in the mentally subnormal children is most overrepresented in lower pregnancy numbers. For the mildly subnormal children, high pregnancy number does not appear to have contributed to low birth weight. In contrast, low birth weight in the severely subnormal children appears to be associated with low pregnancy number.

Gestational Age. It has long been recognized (*cf.* Corner, 1960) that low birth weight is only a crude index of immaturity in the infant. It has been argued with increasing vigor (Neligan, 1965, 1967; Academy of Pediatrics, 1967; Yerushalmy, 1968) that, when considered alone, birth weight can be a misleading indicator in estimating the degree to which a child is at later risk of exhibiting behavioral, intellectual, and neurologic abnormalities. A number of workers (Lubchenko *et al*, 1963) have suggested that a better estimate of a child's immaturity at birth may be obtained if his gestational age is known and can be related to his intrauterine growth achievements. Our intention here is not to enter into the debate over the relative values of birth weight for gestational age, or of their combined influence, but rather to examine the association between gestational age and mental subnormality.

If a gestational age of 38 weeks is taken as the dividing point, it can be seen from Figure 3 that the proportion of mentally subnormal children born before 38 weeks of gestation had been completed was four times as high as was the case in the comparison population. When the distribution of gestational age by weeks for each of the social classes was considered, no social class gradient in the mentally subnormal sample was found, despite the existence of such a gradient in the population as a whole. This finding suggests that in the mentally subnormal group an excess of low gestational ages exists in upper social groupings. Similarly, there was no clear association between gestational age and pregnancy number in the mentally subnormal group.

When the relation of gestational age to the subtypes of mental subnormality was examined (Table 11), a strong relation was found between this variable and some of the subtypes of subnormality. It is of interest that the least excess of children of low gestational age is found in the most severely impaired clinical subgroups. However, even in this group, short gestational age is twice as frequent as in the comparison population. The largest excess of babies of low gestational age is

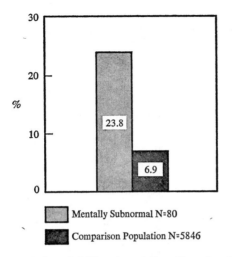

Figure 3. Proportion of children born before 38 weeks of gestation.

found in the intermediate subtypes, either accompanied or unaccompanied by clinical evidence of central nervous system damage. In these groups, five to six times as many children had a gestational age of less than 38 weeks as was the case in the general population. Such children were also in excess in the mildest subtype.

Given the absence of a clear social class gradient for gestational age, as well as the absence of any direct relation between the frequency with which low gestational age occurred and the severity of clinical symptomatology in the mentally subnormal children, it appears likely that short gestation could well be associated with intellectual impairment in general rather than with any specific subvariant of mental subnormality. When taken together with the findings on low birth weight (which was systematically related to severity), these data, although based on very small numbers, suggest the possibility that it is the baby having a low weight for gestational age who will be found in all but the most severely subnormal subtypes. The data in Table 12 support this inference and show that, among infants who are both light in weight and of low gestational age, there is overrepresentation for each clinical subtype. This overrepresentation ranges from a two-fold difference in the most severe subtype to a nine-fold difference in the children with IQs at or above 50 and with evidence of central nervous system damage. Children with normal gestational lengths (38 weeks or more) who weigh less than 6 pounds are three times as frequent in the most severe

TABLE 11.

Relation of gestational age to the subtypes of mental subnormality

Subtype*	Gestational Age (weeks)	Percentage of Children	
		Mentally subnormal	Comparison population
<50; CNS+ (16)	≦36	6.3	3.4†
	37	6.3	3.0†
	38	6.3	6.0†
	39	6.3	14.5†
	40	18.7	24.5†
	41	38.0	27.7†
	≧42	18.7	21.0†
≧50; CNS+ (22)	≦36	31.8	
	37	4.5	
	38	—	
	39	27.3	
	40	9.0	
	41	18.2	
	≧42	9.0	
50–59; CNS− (9)‡	≦38	33.3	
	39	11.1	
	40	11.1	
	41	22.2	
	≧42	22.2	
≧60; CNS− (32)	≦36	12.5	4.1§
	37	6.2	3.3§
	38	—	7.0§
	39	12.5	16.5§
	40	25.0	23.0§
	41	18.8	25.0§
	≧42	25.0	21.0§

* Defined by IQ and presence of central nervous system damage. Figures in parentheses represent the number of cases in each population for which information was available.

† All social classes, 5987 cases.

‡ No cases were ≦37 weeks.

§ Social Classes IV and V, 1796 cases.

TABLE 12.

Relation of gestational age and birth weight to the subtypes of mental sub-normality

Subtype*	Birth Weight (pounds)	Gestational Age (weeks)	Percentage of Children	
			Mentally subnormal	Comparison population
<50; CNS+ (16)	<6	<38	6.2	3.3†
	<6	≧38	25.0	7.9†
	≧6	<38	6.2	3.2†
	≧6	≧38	62.5	85.6†
≧50; CNS+ (22)	<6	<38	31.8	
	<6	≧38	18.2	
	≧6	<38	4.5	
	≧6	≧38	45.5	
50–59; CNS– (9)	<6	<38	22.2	
	<6	≧38	—	
	≧6	<38	11.1	
	≧6	≧38	66.7	
≧60; CNS– (32)	<6	<38	12.5	3.4‡
	<6	≧38	12.5	9.5‡
	≧6	<38	6.3	4.0‡
	≧6	≧38	68.7	83.1‡

* Defined by IQ and presence of central nervous system damage. Figures in parentheses represent the number of cases in each population for which information was available.
† All social classes, 118 cases.
‡ Social Classes IV and V, 34 cases.

subtype and are twice as frequent in the group with IQs above 50 and with clinical signs of central nervous system damage, but they do not occur with elevated frequency in the least severely impaired subgroups as compared with the appropriate comparison populations. Thus, children with both short gestation and low birth weight are the ones over-represented in all subtypes but, at normal gestational age, children with low birth weight are overrepresented in the more severe subtypes.

Condition at Birth. The children of the present study had been classified, as infants, according to a system developed some years ago and reported by Craig and Fraser (1957). The assessment of the baby was made in terms of his condition in the first ½ hour of life. On the basis of the infant's characteristics and requirements for care during this period of observation, he was assigned to one of four classes, designated as A, B, C, and D, which reflected a range from A, fully normal, to B, C, or D, indicating increasing degrees of physiologic disturbance. The criteria used for the placement of an infant within this set of categories are given in Appendix 6.

Determination of the condition of the infant in the 30 minutes following birth had been made for approximately 80 percent of the mentally subnormal children and for approximately 70 percent of the children in the comparison population. The data on the relative frequency with which mentally subnormal children and children in the relevant comparison populations were placed in each of the four classes of condition at birth are presented in Table 13. It was striking to note that only one of the mentally subnormal children had been classified as D—i.e., as being in extremely poor condition. However, when the two lowest conditions, C and D, were combined, it was found that relatively poor condition at birth was noted twice as often in the mentally subnormal children as in the comparison group. When infant status in both the mentally subnormal and comparison populations was considered for social class and parity, no clear gradient was found for these variables.

In Table 14, the relation of infant class to the subtypes of mental subnormality is explored. Children in suboptimal condition at birth, i.e., in Infant Classes C and D, were more frequently present in the three more severely handicapped subgroups of the mentally subnormal children, with one and one-half to six times as high a frequency of children in poor condition at birth in these groups than in the general

TABLE 13.

Distribution by infant class at birth in the mentally subnormal and comparison populations

Infant Class	No. and Percentage of Children			
	Mentally subnormal		Comparison population	
	No.	Percent	No.	Percent
A	58	71.6	4409	78.2
B	14	17.3	923	16.4
C	8	9.9	257	4.5
D	1	1.2	52	0.9
Total	81		5641	

TABLE 14.

Relation of infant class to the subtypes of mental subnormality

Subtype*	Infant Class	Percentage of Children	
		Mentally subnormal	Comparison population
<50; CNS+ (19)	A	73.7	78.2†
	B	15.8	16.4†
	C	10.5	4.5†
	D	—	0.9†
≧50; CNS+ (23)	A	78.3	
	B	13.0	
	C	8.7	
	D	—	
50–59; CNS− (8)	A	62.5	
	B	—	
	C	25.0	
	D	12.5	
≧60; CNS− (30)	A	70.0	80.3‡
	B	26.7	15.1‡
	C	3.3	3.6‡
	D	—	1.0‡

* Defined by IQ and presence of central nervous system damage. Figures in parentheses represent the number of cases in each population for which information was available.

† All social classes, 5641 cases.

‡ Social Classes IV and V, 1628 cases.

population. No such difference was found between the least severely impaired group and its comparison population. These data do not suggest that the status of the infant at birth, as defined by these ratings, was an important risk condition for subnormality.

Since the birth classification of children had been limited to observations carried out during the first ½ hour of extrauterine existence, it provided only a constricted measure of the infant's perinatal condition. A further view of functional disturbances during the perinatal period could, however, be obtained by considering whether sufficient concern over the child's condition existed for him to have been assigned to a special care nursery at some time during the perinatal period. This criterion provides an impure measure of concern, since in Aberdeen practically all babies weighing less than 5.5 pounds are sent to a special nursery, irrespective of their clinical condition. If it is recognized that special nursery assignment, therefore, represents both low birth weight *per se* and the presence of clinical conditions warranting concern, there is some value in looking at special nursery placement as an additional indicator of elevated risk in the perinatal period. An analysis of these children replicated the findings for low birth weight with very few exceptions, which will be considered in the next chapter.

Condition of the Mother

The general health condition and antecedent growth of the mother are, perhaps, more generally pertinent and ubiquitous as determiners of the degree of risk to which the fetus is likely to be exposed than are the more specific complications of pregnancy, labor, and delivery, which may be unique to a particular pregnancy. A variety of studies has demonstrated that strong associations exist between complications of obstetric course as well as abnormalities in the infant and such characteristics of the mother as her age, height, and number of prior pregnancies.

Maternal Age. The maternal age distribution of the mentally subnormal population is almost identical with that of the comparison population. Differences in age are not increased when the clinical subtypes of mental subnormality are considered separately. Therefore, in order to consider the influence of maternal age it is necessary to view it in relation to reproductive history. In studying the influence of age on childbearing, the number of the pregnancy must be taken into account. A woman of 25 may appear as a primapara or as a multipara, with or without a history of previous pregnancy complications, and with any other set of pertinent attributes.

Pregnancy Number. We have already seen that the pregnancy numbers from which the mentally subnormal children come vary both with social class and with subtype of mental subnormality. Different types of pregnancy complication also vary with pregnancy number. Until now, we have been concerned with controlling for this factor. At this point, we shall focus on pregnancy number in its own right and consider it in its relation to maternal age and to the subtypes of mental subnormality.

When one looks at pregnancy number (Table 15), the percentage of first, second, and third pregnancies in the subnormal group (67 percent) was lower than that of the comparison population (81 percent). Con-

TABLE 15.

Distribution of pregnancy numbers characterizing the mothers of the mentally subnormal and comparison populations

Pregnancy No.	Percentage of Children	
	Mentally subnormal*	Comparison population†
1	26.1 ⎫	33.1 ⎫
2	27.2 ⎬ 67.4	29.0 ⎬ 80.5
3	14.1 ⎭	18.4 ⎭
4	12.0	10.0
≧ 5	20.6	9.5

* In 92 cases.
† In 6953 cases.

versely, fifth and higher pregnancy numbers were represented in the mentally subnormal group twice as often as in the comparison population. In the mentally subnormal group, therefore, we have a population of mothers who, although found to be of comparable age with the mothers in the comparison population, have borne more children .

From the analysis presented in Chapter 6, we already know that the mentally subnormal group contains an excess of families from the lower social classes, largely concentrated among the mildly subnormal cases. We may ask, therefore, whether the higher pregnancy number of the subnormal group merely reflects its social composition and the different childbearing habits of the lower socio-economic strata or whether, when social class is controlled, the pregnancy patterns of the mentally subnormal group continue to differ from those of the equivalent social classes in the comparison population. An answer to this question may be obtained by a comparison of number of pregnancies in the different social classes (Table 16). We have evidence that complications of pregnancy are very different in the first two pregnancies than they are in the fifth and subsequent ones. The data on the extremes of pregnancy number by social class show that, with the exception of Social Classes I to IIIa (in which the number of cases is very small), no significant differences in pregnancy number exist between the mentally subnormal group and the comparison population for Social Classes I to IV. The difference between the subnormal group and the comparison population, therefore, appears to have been contributed

TABLE 16.

Extremes of pregnancy number by social class in the mentally subnormal and comparison populations

Pregnancy No.	Percentage of Children in Social Class*							
	I–IIIa		IIIb, IIIc		IV		V	
	Mentally subnormal†	Comparison population	Mentally subnormal‡	Comparison population	Mentally subnormal§	Comparison population	Mentally subnormal¶	Comparison population
1 or 2	66.6	69.8	73.5	64.5	44.4	55.3	38.1	49.1
≧5	16.6	5.6	8.8	7.4	11.1	12.2	33.3	16.1

* Social class not recorded in one case.
† In 6 cases.
‡ In 34 cases.
§ In 9 cases.
¶ In 42 cases.

almost entirely by mothers from Social Class V, in which the percentage of women having five pregnancies or more was twice as high as in the comparison group.

In Table 17, the distribution of pregnancy numbers is shown for the subtypes of mental subnormality and the comparison population. Children with IQs of less than 50 and with clinical evidence of central nervous system damage are the only subtype overrepresented in the first pregnancies. In contrast, the least handicapped mentally subnormal are slightly underrepresented in the low pregnancy numbers and are overrepresented in pregnancy numbers four or greater. This difference is illustrated in Figure 4.

The data suggest strongly that pregnancy number and social class are interrelated and are conjointly associated with mental subnormality as a whole and with its subtypes. Moreover, a fuller consideration must also include maternal age. This issue will be considered in greater detail in the next chapter.

Maternal Height. Over the years a considerable body of data has demonstrated a relationship between reproductive performance and maternal height. In summarizing certain of these findings, Illsley (1967) has pointed out that:

...for many years the evidence relating stature to reproductive performance rested on a series of reports from Baird and his colleagues in Aberdeen (Baird, 1952, 1962; Bernard, 1952; Illsley, 1953; Baird & Thomson, 1954;

TABLE 17.

Relation of pregnancy number to the subtypes of mental subnormality

Subtype*	Pregnancy No.	Percentage of Children	
		Mentally subnormal	Comparison population
<50; CNS+ (20)	1	50	33.1†
	2	35	29.0†
	3	5	18.4†
	4	—	10.0†
	≧5	10	9.5†
≧50; CNS+ (24)	1	16.7	
	2	33.3	
	3	20.8	
	4	12.5	
	≧5	16.7	
50–59; CNS− (10)	1	20	
	2	30	
	3	20	
	4	20	
	≧5	10	
≧60; CNS− (37)	1	18.9	25.7‡
	2	18.9	26.2‡
	3	13.5	20.3‡
	4	16.2	12.7‡
	≧5	32.4	15.0‡

* Defined by IQ and presence of central nervous system damage. Figures in parentheses represent the number of cases in each population for which information was available.

† All social classes, 6953 cases.

‡ Social Classes IV and V, 2062 cases.

Stewart & Bernard, 1954; Thomson, 1959). These studies showed a strong and continuous association between height and perinatal death, birth weight, pelvic distortion, difficult delivery, and birth trauma. More recently similar evidence has been reported by other observers.

Positive relationships between maternal height and birth weight and/or prematurity have been reported from England (Martin, 1954), Scotland (Drillien, 1957), Philadelphia (Kasius *et al*, 1958), South Africa (Stein & Susser, 1958), Hong Kong (Thomson & Billewicz, 1963), and a highly heterogeneous group of hospitals and clinics in

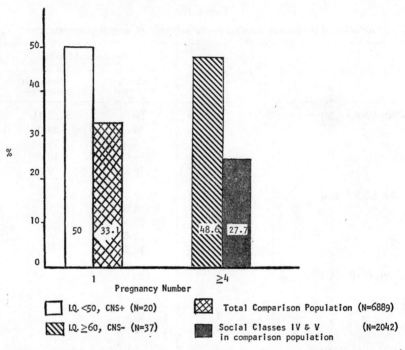

Figure 4. The relation of pregnancy number to the most and least severe sub-types of mental subnormality.

underdeveloped areas participating in a world-wide study of low birth weight (Crosse, 1960), as well as the hospital groups participating in the collaborative study of the causes of central nervous system damage which have been organized by the National Institute of Neurological Diseases and Blindness. The Perinatal Mortality Survey of Great Britain (Butler & Bonham, 1963), using a national sample of nearly 17,000 births and 8000 perinatal deaths, demonstrates perinatal mortality ratios (mean for Great Britain = 100) of 79 for women of 65 inches or more, rising to 114 for women of 62 inches or less. Detailed inspection of the data reveals much wider and consistent variation when the full range of heights is employed (Illsley, 1967).

Moreover, Thomson (p. 651, 1956), in reviewing the Aberdeen data, has concluded that "most short women are not genetically small, but have been made so by conditions experienced during growth." He has suggested too, that certain of the reproductive difficulties experienced by the short women may derive not only from the smallness of their stature and from possible pelvic deformities but also from the clear association which exists in any community between low stature, low social status, and poor conditions of general health.

In view of the relation between the stature of women and their reproductive performance, we have examined the extent to which differences in the heights of mothers were associated with the presence of mental subnormality in their children. The data presented in Figure 5 summarize our findings both when the mothers of the mentally subnormal group as a whole are compared with the population from which they were drawn and when the mothers of the mentally subnormal group and mothers in the general population are compared within social classes. As may be seen from this figure, if a height of 5 feet is taken as the dividing point, a slight excess of the shorter women is found among the mothers of the mentally subnormal group. However, a consideration

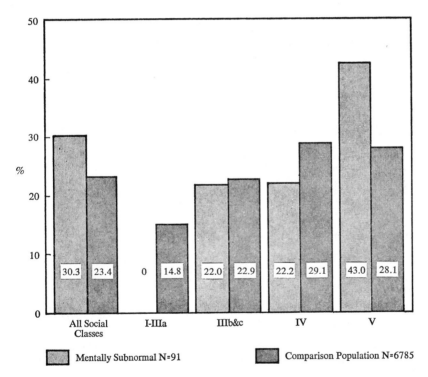

Figure 5. The relative frequency of very short mothers ($\leqq$ 60 inches) in the mentally subnormal and comparison populations.

of this finding by social class indicates that the only social class in which the mothers of mentally subnormal children are in significant excess for short stature is Social Class V. For all other social class groupings, a small and nonsignificant difference in the opposite direction exists.

When maternal height is considered in each of the subtypes (Table 18 and Figure 6), it is notable that very short women are clearly underrepresented among the mothers of the most severely impaired children. Only 5 percent of these mothers are at or under 60 inches in height as compared with 23 percent of the mothers in the comparison population. Conversely, short stature is overrepresented among mothers in the least severe subtype of mental subnormality, with 46 percent of them of low stature as compared with 29 percent in the relevant segment of the comparison population.

Taken as a whole, the data suggest that the mothers of mentally sub-

TABLE 18.

Relation of maternal height to the subtypes of mental subnormality

Subtype*	Maternal Height (inches)	Percentage of Children	
		Mentally subnormal	Comparison population
<50; CNS+ (20)	≦60	5.0	23.1†
	61–63	70.0	49.6†
	≧64	25.0	27.3†
≧50; CNS+ (23)	≦60	26.1	
	61–63	39.1	
	≧64	34.8	
50–59; CNS− (9)	≦60	22.2	
	61–63	44.4	
	≧64	33.3	
≧60; CNS− (37)	≦60	45.9	28.9‡
	61–63	45.9	50.4‡
	≧64	8.1	20.7‡

* Defined by IQ and presence of central nervous system damage. Figures in parentheses represent the number of cases in each population for which information was available.

† All social classes, 6889 cases.

‡ Social Classes IV and V, 2042 cases.

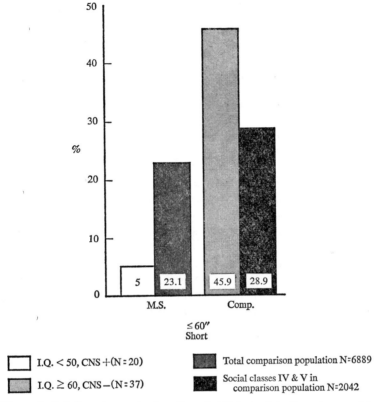

Figure 6. Relation of very short mothers (≦ 60 inches) to the extreme subtypes of mental subnormality.

normal children belonging to the subtype with IQs of 60 or more and with no clinical evidence of central nervous system damage contained almost twice as many short women as did mothers of normal children in the same social classes. Conversely, there is a five-fold underrepresentation of short women among the mothers of the most severely subnormal children as compared with the total population.

An analysis was also made of the relation between the height of the mothers in the mentally subnormal group and the presence of disturbances in obstetric and perinatal course. Findings similar to those that have been previously reported were found between the height of the mother and the infant's birth weight. Most important, however, from the obstetric viewpoint was the finding that the height of the mother bore a significant relationship to the condition of the infant at birth, with babies in poor condition (Classes C and D) more frequent when the mothers were less than 5 feet in height ($\chi^2 = 5.58$; p $<$ .025, Yates correction applied). These findings, taken together with the analyses in Chapters 6 and 7, suggest that the children in the mildest clinical subtype of mental subnormality are exposed to a combination of maternal, obstetric, and social factors for risk in their development.

A variety of other characteristics of the mothers, including physical grade and previous reproductive history, may influence the course of the present pregnancy. These factors are considered in Chapter 9.

Summary

Our consideration of the general associations between mental subnormality and factors related to pregnancy, birth, and perinatal status has indicated that certain types of perinatal complications were present significantly more frequently in the mentally subnormal group than in the comparison population. Preeclamptic toxemia of moderate and severe degree, low birth weight, short gestation, and poor condition in the perinatal period were all present more frequently in the mentally subnormal group than in the general population. The complications of delivery that clearly were more frequently present in the mentally subnormal group were breech and other malpresentations and multiple births. Abnormalities in the duration of labor, assisted deliveries, and cesarean sections were not overrepresented in the mentally subnormal group. However, cases in the intermediate subtypes did show an excess of very short labors.

Obstetric and perinatal complications were not uniformly associated with all subtypes of subnormality. Children who had associated findings of central nervous system damage on clinical examination tended to be the ones in whom such complications were overrepresented.

An analysis of the characteristics of the mother as a reproducer indicated that short mothers with high pregnancy numbers were overrepresented in mild subnormality and that mothers with low pregnancy numbers tended to be overrepresented in cases in which intellectual handicap was severe and was accompanied by central nervous system damage.

The relative absence of conditions of definable obstetric and perinatal risk coupled with the presence of generally poor physical condition in the mother and low birth weight in the child for the least severely impaired children leave little ground for attributing a primary obstetric etiology for mental subnormality in these cases. Rather, the findings suggest that the handicap is most likely to have derived from an interaction of social-environmental circumstances, familial factors, and ill-defined features of reproductive inadequacy.

Clearly, many of the associations of mental subnormality with complications of pregnancy and pathology of the neonate, as well as with such factors as family size, ordinality, and pregnancy number, may be attributable, at least in part, to differences in the fertility patterns and physical attributes found in the different social classes. To sort out these relationships in the mentally subnormal group requires an analysis in depth of each case and of appropriate controls in terms of associated familial, obstetric, and neonatal characteristics. It is to such an analysis that we now turn in Chapter 9.

9

An Intensive Clinical Consideration of Births Resulting in Mentally Subnormal Children

In the previous chapter, we compared the frequency of occurrence of obstetric complications in the mentally subnormal group with that in the total population from which it is drawn. We noted a higher prevalence of a variety of complications, including preeclampsia, breech delivery, and low birth weight. However, we cannot conclude from such evidence that these complications *caused* damage to the child's central nervous system or were responsible for the mental subnormality. We have already noted that some of the obstetric factors often presumed to be relevant in the etiology of subnormality, such as prematurity, occur more frequently in some social classes or subtypes of subnormality than in others and that their statistical association with subnormality may reflect the different social incidence of both the complications and the subnormality, rather than a true causal link. We also know that, in the total population, there were many cases of preeclampsia, low birth weight, and the like, and that only very few of the children exposed to such complications were mentally subnormal. Thus, we may ask whether these complications were particularly severe in the case of the mentally subnormal children or whether, in such cases, there were several complications rather than just one. It may be hypothesized, for example, that preeclampsia or low birth weight may be relatively unimportant if either occurs alone, but that the consequences are more serious when they occur together. Similarly, poor intrauterine growth may render a child particularly susceptible to postnatal infection or injury in some environmental circumstances but may be much more readily compensated by good care and nutrition in others. For these reasons a careful analysis of all of the available obstetric and social data for the mentally subnormal group is needed on a case study basis, so that one can assess the severity of each complication and its possible consequences for the child's neurologic and intellectual development. Once this analysis is made and the findings are quantified, the complications of pregnancy and delivery, the health and physique of the mother, the social status of the family, and the intellectual abilities of the subnormal child's siblings can be systematically related to the intelligence and neurologic status of the child.

We do not wish to provide a detailed case analysis for each of the subnormal children in our series. However illuminating this information might be, the result would be extremely tedious, and generalization would be difficult. We wish, rather, to derive from our case material evidence of the interrelationships between such various factors as appear to have etiologic significance so that we may make higher order generalizations about the contribution of various obstetric complications to the causation of different types and degrees of mental subnormality. With the small population of subnormal children in this study, it will frequently be impossible to show the relationships between obstetric events and clinical subtypes of mental subnormality for each social class and for each birth order and family size—all of which are characteristics that have been shown to be epidemiologically significant. Those epidemiologic associations discussed in the previous chapter, therefore, have to be borne in mind constantly. Thus, we have seen that the lowest social classes were heavily overrepresented in the subnormal population and that, within these classes, there was an excess of high parity births. At all parities and in the lowest social classes, the mothers of mentally subnormal children were shorter in stature than those of the comparison population, and the short stature was accompanied in many cases by poor general health and physique, as these were assessed by the obstetricians who cared for the mothers during pregnancy and delivery.

Equally important differences were found among the subtypes. The severely subnormal group did not differ from the comparison population in social class or high pregnancy number. The mild subtype did show such a difference, however, and the excessive representation of the lowest social classes and high parities was particularly marked in this group. Thus, when results are shown for higher pregnancy numbers, we are automatically considering a predominantly lower class group in which the mildly subnormal are overrepresented. Similarly, in talking of an upper class group, we are presenting data on a group characterized by low pregnancy numbers and heavily weighted toward the severely subnormal. Because of these associations, wherever possible, we shall consider our findings in relation to subtypes of subnormality, pregnancy numbers, and social class. Since breaking down the population into five social classes results in very small numbers, we have decided to divide the population into two broad social groupings—manual and nonmanual.

As in the last chapter, analysis of the mentally subnormal children is based on 92 cases and excludes children with Down's Syndrome, nonresidents, those not born in Aberdeen, and one postencephalitic case. Wherever appropriate, comparison was made with a small random sample (126 children) of the non-handicapped population, whose case records were examined in similar detail. In all cases the detailed evaluation of case histories was undertaken by one member of the team (D. B.) who, in reaching his conclusions on obstetric and perinatal factors, was unaware of the subtype of mental subnormality to which the child belonged. However, he was aware of whether the case considered was a mentally subnormal child or a control. Throughout this chapter, therefore, the terms "upper social group" and "lower social group" refer respectively to Social Classes I to IIIb (composed of nonmanual and skilled tradesmen) and IIIc to V (other skilled, semiskilled, and unskilled manual workers).

Scoring the Case Records

For an assessment of obstetric complications, each case history was examined in detail and a marking system was employed in which the highest score signified the greatest severity. The maximal score is 12, with 4 points each alloted for pregnancy, labor, and the neonatal condition of the child. The rationale behind the attempt to attach a score to the degree of severity of the complication was as follows. The consultant obstetrician attempted a three-fold classification of the severity of each and every complication which was recorded in the case notes. A complication was assigned to the category "of doubtful or minor significance" if, in the obstetrician's judgment, the difficulty was slight but could not be entirely ignored. Such cases were given a score of 1. If, however, the complication was rather more serious, but still not of major significance, the case was placed in an intermediate category and assigned a score of 2. These types or degrees of severity may be thought of as causing concern rather than anxiety at the time.

The third category was regarded as both qualitatively and quantitatively more serious. In these cases, clear and definite risk was involved and this markedly greater degree of severity, it was felt, should be reflected in the scoring. Thus, a score of 4 was assigned rather than 3.

The following examples illustrate these distinctions.

Pregnancy Score. (Preeclampsia as an example.)

1. Rise of blood pressure in pregnancy with little or no edema and never more than a trace of albumin in the urine. Blood pressure usually settles quickly with rest in bed in hospital. Patient may continue with the pregnancy and attend as an outpatient.

2. Blood pressure higher (more than 150/100) with definite edema and albumin up to 2 g. per liter in the urine. Surgical induction usually performed about the 37th or 38th week.

4. Blood pressure usually higher still and more than 2 g. per liter of albumin in the urine. Usually labor has to be inducted for the sake of the mother, even before the 37th week in some cases, or because the baby is not growing.

Labor Score.

1. Delivery by forceps because of delay in the second stage of labor, weak uterine contractions, or inadequate bearing-down efforts by the mother.

2. More difficult delivery because of a big baby or occiput posterior position of the fetus requiring turning. There may be some irregularity of the fetal heart in the second stage or meconium may be passed into the liquor amnii.

4. Prolonged labor (first as well as second stage). Forceps delivery requiring a strong pull. Sometimes evidence of disproportion as shown by overmolding of the fetal head. The same gradation in the amount of difficulty can occur with other abnormalities, such as breech presentation.

Child Score.

1. Child unable to breathe at once despite the absence of sedation of the mother. Mucus removed from the throat and oxygen given by mask. Very quick recovery.

2. More delay in breathing with possibly poor color, some cardiac irregularity, and poor muscle tone. Sometimes there is considerable delay in breathing which may be attributable to the effect of sedation or to the administration of general anesthesia. Intubation may be required but response is good and, especially if the child weighs more than 2500 g., admission to special nursery may not be necessary.

4. a. Child limp at birth and there may be considerable delay in response. There may be signs of cerebral irritation and cyanotic attacks.

b. In a small baby, there may be indrawing of the chest and cyanosis may return after removal from incubator and continuous oxygen. c. There may be deep jaundice by about the fourth day with other signs of a high bilirubin blood content.

Assessment of Risk

The object of the scoring system is to ensure that pathologic conditions are not overlooked although they may not have an effect on the baby. For example, it is well-known that a rise of blood pressure during pregnancy has no effect by itself on the birth weight of the baby. Again, "severe preeclampsia" may be registered because of a sudden rise of blood pressure and development of large quantities of albumin in the urine at about 38 weeks' gestation. In such cases, induction of labor is performed after a short period of sedation and, unless there are other complications in labor, such as accidental hemorrhage, the baby is usually unaffected. This situation accounts for the fact that the "prematurity" rate in cases of moderate and mild preeclampsia is very low, the explanation being that this rise of blood pressure usually occurs late in pregnancy and, thus, most of those likely to go into premature labor have already done so. The type of case in which preeclampsia may have an effect is one in which the albumin $(++)$ occurs much earlier in pregnancy (e.g., 33 weeks), when the baby is still small. After the appearance of the albumin in large amounts, fetal growth usually ceases and, if labor is not induced, intrauterine death occurs. Thus, there are two types of severe preeclampsia.

Clearly, the short, undernourished woman from one of the lower social classes, who tends to have a small baby even at term, is much more likely to have her baby damaged by severe preeclampsia, especially if the condition begins early in pregnancy. Again, the big baby who scores high marks in labor but responds well to treatment at birth and gives no further cause for anxiety would seem to have less risk of permanent damage than one who has a relapse within a few hours or days of delivery, whether or not there were high marks in pregnancy and labor. In such cases the baby is likely to be badly grown or premature. Thus, it could be argued that if an experienced obstetrician took into account all of these various factors of pregnancy or labor, as well as the response of the child, and gave his estimate of the chances of damage, he might be nearer the truth than if he simply took the scores at their face value. This type of estimation has been done in the present study. In addition, the actual scores have been given.

The following case, for example, would justify a maximal severity score of 12:

Severe preeclampsia occurring sufficiently early in pregnancy to
    interfere with fetal growth   4 points
Prolapse of the umbilical cord during labor resulting in gross ir-
    regularity of the fetal heart   4 points
Asphyxia of the baby at birth requiring intubation and prolonged
    administration of oxygen   4 points.

After all of the case notes for both mentally subnormal and comparison groups had been examined and scored according to this scheme, average total "severity" scores were calculated for each social class. Table 1 shows that the mean severity score of the mentally subnormal group (2.5) is markedly higher than that of the comparison group (1.2). Differences of the same order of magnitude occur within social classes as well as overall. There is a particularly high score in Social Classes I and II. It should be noted, however, that we are dealing with small numbers in the higher social classes so that the score of 6.0 for this group may be specific to this sample.

The severity scores of the mentally subnormal children are also higher than those of the comparison group at each pregnancy number (see Table 2), but the difference is most striking in second and third pregnancies. It is interesting to note that the comparison group shows the expected pattern of scores, namely, a highest score in first pregnancies, a low score in second and third pregnancies, and a score rising

TABLE 1.

Distribution of mean total obstetric severity scores by current social class in mentally subnormal and comparison populations

| | No. of Children and Mean Severity Score | | | |
| Social Class | Mentally subnormal | | Comparison population | |
	No.	Score	No.	Score
I, II	3	6.0		
IIIa	3	2.5	31	1.4
IIIb	14	1.7	23	1.0
IIIc	20	3.1	31	1.2
IV, V, and others	52	2.4	41	1.1
Total or mean	92	2.5	126	1.2

TABLE 2.

Distribution of mean total obstetric severity scores by pregnancy number in mentally subnormal and comparison populations

| Pregnancy No. | No. of Children and Mean Severity Score | | | |
| | Mentally subnormal | | Comparison population | |
	No.	Score	No.	Score
1	24	3.3	41	1.6
2	26	2.8	38	0.8
3	12	2.4	24	0.6
≧4	30	1.7	23	1.1
Total or mean	92	2.5	126	1.2

again for fourth and later pregnancies. By contrast, the mentally subnormal group is characterized by a fall in severity score at each pregnancy number. We shall return to this point later in the chapter.

The disparity between the groups is evident for each of the three components of score—pregnancy, labor, and child (Table 3). It is particularly noticeable in second and third pregnancies and is least pronounced for labor. The marked difference between the mentally subnormal and comparison groups in severity scores in pregnancy but not in labor suggests that pregnancy may be of more importance than labor in causing damage to the child. Furthermore, the similarity of the trends of the scores for pregnancy and for condition as a newborn suggests that the two may be interrelated. Of course, it is possible that,

TABLE 3.

Distribution of mean obstetric severity scores in pregnancy, labor, and child by pregnancy number

| Stage | Mean Severity Score of Mentally Subnormal Children at Pregnancy No. | | | | | Mean Severity Score of Comparison Population at Pregnancy No. | | | | |
	1	2	3	≧4	All	1	2	3	≧4	All
Pregnancy...	1.1	1.1	1.1	0.7	1.0	0.8	0.3	0.2	0.3	0.4
Labor.......	1.1	0.6	0.5	0.5	0.7	0.5	0.4	0.3	0.3	0.4
Child.......	1.1	1.0	0.8	0.5	0.8	0.3	0.2	0.2	0.5	0.4
Total.......	3.3	2.7	2.4	1.7	2.5	1.6	0.9	0.7	1.1	1.2

in some cases at least, a high score for exposure to risk in the newborn period indicates a basic fetal defect which made the infant less able to stand up to the stress of even a normal labor.

The hypothesis of obstetric damage would be greatly strengthened if, within the mentally subnormal group, high severity scores were concentrated in children with associated signs of central nervous system damage. Table 4 shows that severity scores are indeed higher for children with positive neurologic signs (3.0, as against 2.1). This statement, however, requires considerable qualification.

1. It does not apply to any component in fourth and later pregnancies nor to labor in a third pregnancy.

2. The CNS− cases themselves have considerably higher severity scores than does the comparison group (see previous table). The mean scores for CNS+, CNS−, and comparison groups are respectively 3.0, 2.0, and 1.2. The same ranking of scores applies to the scores for pregnancy, labor, and child, and for first, second, and third pregnancies. For fourth and later pregnancies the ranking changes, however, and there is a sharp contrast between, on the one hand, CNS− (2.1) and, on the other, CNS+ (1.0) and the comparison group (1.1). These data suggest that it is possible to have a group with high severity scores which has no accompanying clinical signs of central nervous system damage. However, the number of CNS+ cases in the higher pregnancy numbers is too small to warrant a firm conclusion.

From the analysis presented in previous chapters we know that the upper social group children are mainly in the CNS+ category, whereas the CNS− group is weighted toward the lower social classes. We need to know to what extent the relationship between severity scores and

TABLE 4.

Relation of mean obstetric severity scores in pregnancy, labor, and child to associated signs of central nervous system damage

Stage	Mean Severity Score of CNS+ Children at Pregnancy No.					Mean Severity Score of CNS− Children at Pregnancy No.				
	1	2	3	≧4	All	1	2	3	≧4	All
Pregnancy...	1.3	1.3	1.3	0.4	1.1	0.9	0.7	0.9	0.9	0.9
Labor.......	1.4	0.7	0.3	0.0	0.7	0.8	0.3	0.4	0.7	0.6
Child.......	1.5	1.2	1.3	0.6	1.2	0.7	0.7	0.3	0.5	0.6
Total.......	4.2	3.2	2.9	1.0	3.0	2.4	1.7	1.6	2.1	2.1

associated signs of central nervous system damage is affected by the association of the latter with social class. Does the CNS+ group have higher severity scores within a social class than does the CNS− group? If it does not, we would have reason to question the causal significance of severity scores. The mean severity score for all subnormal children of the upper class group (2.3) is slightly lower than that of the lower class group (2.6) (Table 5). However, we can see that, although the numbers are too small for firm conclusions, the mean score of the CNS+ group within the upper social group is considerably higher than that of the CNS− children. Within the lower social class we can also make comparisons. In first, second, and third pregnancies, the mean severity score of the CNS+ children (4.3) is almost twice as high as in the equivalent upper social class (2.6) and again is much higher than that of CNS− in the lower social class (2.1). In fourth or later pregnancies, however, CNS+ children have very low severity scores (0.7).

The broad relationship between severity scores and associated signs of central nervous system damage holds within classes. Over all pregnancy numbers, the CNS+ children have a mean score of 2.4 against the 1.0 of the CNS− children in the upper social group, while, in the lower class group, the scores are respectively 3.4 and 2.1. The highest severity scores occur, therefore, in the lower class and in lower pregnancy numbers of the CNS+ category (4.3), in which the mean score

TABLE 5.

Distribution of mean total obstetric severity scores by social group, pregnancy number, and central nervous system diagnosis

Social Group	Pregnancy No.	No. of Children and Mean Severity Score					
		CNS+		CNS−		All	
		No.	Score	No.	Score	No.	Score
Upper	1–3	16	2.6	3	1.0	19	2.4
	≧4	1	0	0	0	1	0
	Total or mean	17	2.4	3	1.0	20	2.3
Lower	1–3	21	4.3	22	2.1	43	3.2
	≧4	7	0.7	22	2.0	29	1.7
	Total or mean	28	3.4	44	2.1	72	2.6
Total or mean	All	45	3.0	47	2.0	92	2.5

is twice as high as in the equivalent class and pregnancy groups of the CNS− category.

The mean severity score, of course, includes many cases where no obstetric complications occurred and thus have been given a zero score. It is possible that the inclusion of such cases has obscured a sharper relationship between neurologic status and severity of complications in those cases where such complications did occur.

In Table 6, therefore, we have set out the cases which had a zero score according to central nervous system diagnosis, pregnancy number, and social class grouping. It can be seen that approximately one-third of cases in both CNS+ and CNS− categories had no significant complications. Unless we are dealing with unrecognized or unrecorded types of complication, therefore, the neurologic damage was caused by factors other than the noted ones in at least one-third of the cases. At the same time it should be noted that the highest proportion of zero scores occurred in the lower social class and in the fourth or later pregnancies. If we omit children with zero severity scores, we are left with 30 CNS+ and 31 CNS− children with a score of at least 1. The mean scores of these children are shown in Table 7. The mean scores are, of course, higher than those which included the cases with zero score, but the difference between the scores of the CNS+ and the CNS− groups has remained proportionately the same, the former being one and one-

TABLE 6.

Distribution of zero obstetric severity scores by current social class, pregnancy number, and central nervous system diagnosis

Social Class	Pregnancy No.	No. and Percentage of Children								
		CNS+			CNS−			All		
		No. mentally sub-normal	No. with zero score	Percent	No. mentally sub-normal	No. with zero score	Percent	No. mentally sub-normal	No. with zero score	Percent
I–IIIb	1–3	16	5	31	3	0	0	19	5	26
	≧4	1	1	100	0	—	—	1	1	100
IIIc–V	1–3	21	3	14	22	5	23	43	8	19
	≧4	7	6	86	22	11	50	29	17	59
Total	All	45	15	33	47	16	34	92	31	34

TABLE 7.

Distribution of mean total obstetric scores of cases with obstetric complications by current social class, pregnancy number, and central nervous system diagnosis

Social Class	Pregnancy No.	No. of Children and Mean Severity Score					
		CNS+		CNS−		All	
		No.	Score	No.	Score	No.	Score
I–IIIb	1–3	11	3.8	3	1.0	14	3.2
	≧4	0	—	0	—	0	—
IIIc–V	1–3	18	5.0	17	2.8	35	3.9
	≧4	1	5.0	11	4.1	12	4.2
Total or mean	All	30	4.6	31	3.1	61	3.8

half times as great as the latter. However, the differences by pregnancy number in the lower class group have now changed, with the later pregnancies, although fewer in number, having the highest severity scores. In other words, while more than one-half of the fourth or later pregnancies were uncomplicated and thus had zero scores, the remainder were sufficiently difficult to raise the severity scores above the average for the lower pregnancy numbers. All but one of the 12 later pregnancies which were complicated, however, are in the CNS− category. This evidence suggests, therefore, that, at least in this population of subnormal children, those complications which are associated with multiparity do not appear to produce clinically identifiable findings of central nervous system damage. In the earlier pregnancies, by contrast, the scores of the CNS+ children are markedly higher than those of the CNS− children, and the possibility of a causal link between these obstetric complications and neurologic damage remains.

Thus far, we have confined ourselves to an analysis of mean scores for the various subgroups of the mentally subnormal population. It is possible, however, that a severity score of 4 deriving from an accumulation of minor complications at each stage may differ in its effects from a similar score resulting from severe adversity at one stage only. In Table 8, therefore, we show the number of children receiving a maximal severity score at any stage. This analysis reveals a marked difference between CNS+ and CNS− children. Of the 31 CNS− children with a severity score above zero, only 5 (16 percent) received a maximal score at any stage, compared with 15 of 30 (50 percent) among the

TABLE 8.

Distribution of cases with maximal severity score (4) at any stage by current social class and central nervous system diagnosis

Neurologic Status	Social Class	No. of Children Affected at Stage				
		Pregnancy	Labor	Child	All stages*	
					1	2
CNS+	I–IIIb	1	1	2	11	4
	IIIc–V	7	3	6	19	11
CNS–	I–IIIb	—	—	—	3	—
	IIIc–V	3	2	2	28	5

* Since some children received maximal scores at more than one stage, the figure in this column refers to the number of children involved and not to the number of maximal scores recorded; 1, no. of cases with severity score >1; 2, no. of cases with maximal score (4).

CNS+ children. More than any of the other measures shown previously, this one seems to be indicative of an association between obstetric events and neurologic damage. It may also be noted that the association is somewhat stronger in the lower social groups than in the upper ones.

We may summarize this part of our findings as follows:

1. The mentally subnormal children are characterized by more obstetric abnormality than a comparison group but not all subnormal children, even those who are CNS+, have evidence of such complications;

2. The excess, although present for all pregnancy numbers, seems particularly characteristic of second and third pregnancies, in which it is evidenced more by the incidence of complications in pregnancy and the child than by complications of labor;

3. Obstetric and neonatal complications, particularly of the more severe kind, are greater in the CNS+ children.

Examination of Specific Complications

Pregnancy. Analysis by severity scores has revealed a general relationship between neurologic status in mental subnormality and obstetric complications. On the other hand, the aggregation into a single severity score of different types of complications with differing degrees of severity cannot reveal the etiologic processes through which this rela-

TABLE 9.

Distribution of antenatal complications by pregnancy number in mentally subnormal and comparison populations

Complication	No. of Children at Pregnancy No.							
	1		2 and 3		≧4		Total	
	Mentally subnormal	Comparison population	Mentally subnormal	Comparison population	Mentally subnormal	Comparison population	Mentally subnormal	Comparison population
High blood pressure + mild preeclampsia......	6	14	1	5	0	0	7	19
Moderate preeclampsia...	3	1	1	0	0	0	4	1
Severe preeclampsia......	2	1	5	2	0	0	7	3
Antepartum hemorrhage..	0	2	4	2	3	1	7	5
Threatened abortion......	1	1	3	1	0	0	4	2
Urinary infection.........	1	2	1	1	0	0	2	3
Low weight gain..........	1	0	1	0	0	0	2	0
Anemia + debility.......	0	0	3	0	7	2	10	2
Rh incompatibility.......	0	0	1	0	0	0	1	0
Others.................	1	1	1	0	0	0	2	1
No. of complications.....	15	22	21	11	10	3	46	36
Total no. of women.......	24	41	38	62	30	23	92	126
Percent*.................	58	54	58	18	33	13	50	29

* Some cases had more than one complication and are therefore represented more than once; percent, no. of complications/total no. of women.

tionship is established. We turn now, therefore, to a consideration of the particular complications arising at each stage. Table 9 sets out the complications of pregnancy in the mentally subnormal and comparison populations. Taking all pregnancies together, the frequency of complications is much higher in the mentally subnormal group than in the comparison population (50 percent against 29 percent). This excess is largely attributable to three groups of complications—moderate and severe preeclampsia, antepartum hemorrhage and threatened abortion, and maternal anemia and debility.

The incidence of complications in the comparison group is high in first pregnancies and falls sharply in subsequent pregnancies. In the mentally subnormal group the incidence is also high in first pregnancies but is even higher in second and third pregnancies; in fourth and later pregnancies the rate falls but is still higher than in the comparison group. The excess of complications in the second and third pregnancies clearly is very largely responsible for the overall difference between the mentally subnormal and comparison groups.

We know that a moderate rise of blood pressure without proteinuria, recorded in Table 9 as high blood pressure or mild preeclampsia, does not increase the risk of perinatal death or even reduce the birth weight of the baby (Baird *et al*, 1957). However, should the blood pressure rise higher and be accompanied by edema and the presence of albumin in the urine, the outlook is more serious, especially if this condition occurs before the 36th week of pregnancy. Such cases are labeled as either moderate or severe preeclampsia, depending on the height of the blood pressure and the amount of albumin in the urine. Table 9 shows that, in first pregnancies in the mentally subnormal group, there were 11 cases with a raised blood pressure, of whom five came into the category "moderate or severe preeclampsia." In the comparison group, only two of the 16 primigravidae with a raised blood pressure fell into the moderate or severe category. The excess of moderate and severe preeclampsia in the mentally subnormal cases was even greater in second and third pregnancies. Since severe preeclampsia is very largely a disease of first pregnancies (MacGillivray, 1958), the high prevalence of this complication in second and third pregnancies in the mentally subnormal group is of particular interest and may be of some importance in the causation of handicap. This possibility is strengthened by the fact that all mentally subnormal children deriving from pregnancies with severe preeclampsia showed signs of central nervous system damage (Table 10). On the other hand, it will be seen from Table 11 that *in five of the seven cases, severe preeclampsia occurred in combination with other potentially damaging complications and circumstances.*

Although there must be a presumption that severe preeclampsia carries a high risk of damage, it cannot be concluded whether, in itself, it has a direct effect on the child or whether it acts through its association with such factors as twinning, low birth weight, and mechanical causes of difficult labor.

The 11 cases of antepartum hemorrhage and threatened abortion were divided almost equally between the CNS+ and CNS− groups, and Table 10 reveals that no other complication of pregnancy occurred disproportionately in the CNS+ cases. There is, however, a marked excess of anemia and debility in the CNS− cases, particularly in those having four pregnancies or more—a finding which suggests a poor level of health and nutrition in the women in this parity group.

There is also the important problem of twin pregnancies. In five cases resulting in mentally subnormal children, the pregnancy was compli-

TABLE 10.

Distribution of antenatal complications by parity and neurologic status

Complication	No. of CNS+ Children at Pregnancy No.		No. of CNS− Children at Pregnancy No.		Total
	1–3	≧4	1–3	≧4	
High blood pressure + mild pre-eclampsia...................	2		5		7
Moderate preeclampsia...........	2		2		4
Severe preeclampsia.............	7				7
Antepartum hemorrhage..........	2	1	2	2	7
Threatened abortion.............	3		1		4
Twin pregnancy.................	4			1	5
Anemia + debility..............	1		2	7	10
Others.........................	5		2		7
Total.........................	26	1	14	10	51

TABLE 11.

Distribution of complications associated with severe preeclampsia

No. of Children	Pregnancy No.	Other Complications and Circumstances
2	1	—
	1	Twin pregnancy, 2nd twin, prolapse of cord, forceps delivery, birth weight 5 pounds
4	2	—
	2	Threatened abortion
	2	Multiple fibroids, breech delivery, birth weight 2 pounds 15 ounces
	2	Twin pregnancy, 2nd twin, internal version, breech delivery, birth weight 4 pounds 6 ounces
1	3	Illegitimate, no antenatal care, eclampsia, mother died
Total 7		

cated by the presence of twins. Four of these five had positive obstetric severity scores, and all of these four had associated signs of neurologic damage. The mean severity scores of the four pregnancies were 2.3, 1.5, and 3.3 respectively for pregnancy, labor, and child. In one case, the maximal score of 12 was given, and the other three had the maximal score of 4 either for pregnancy or for the neonatal condition of the child. Two of the pregnancies were complicated by severe preeclampsia and another, by antepartum hemorrhage. One child was delivered by forceps, while another was delivered by the breech. In three cases, the mentally subnormal child was the smaller twin and, in the fourth, both babies weighed under 4 pounds at birth.

These twin pregnancies, although forming only a small proportion of the total population of mentally subnormal children, occur in combination with other complications and are thus disproportionately represented in the total list of complications.

Labor. The type of labor and delivery experienced by the mentally subnormal and comparison groups is shown in Table 12. There are slight differences between the two groups in the relative proportions of deliveries in less than 24 hours and over 24 hours, with the mentally subnormal group being somewhat overrepresented in the longer labors. As was shown in Chapter 8, this difference is not significant, however, and labor lasted over 24 hours in only four of the mentally subnormal cases.

The main differences lie not so much in the duration of labor as in the excess of instrumental deliveries in the mentally subnormal group—

TABLE 12.

Distribution of children affected by duration of labor and method of delivery

| Maternal Status and Population | No. of Children Affected by | | | | | |
| | Duration of labor (hours) | | Type of presentation or delivery | | | |
	<24	≧24	Spontaneous	Forceps	Breech	Cesarean section
Primiparae						
Mentally subnormal.....	21	2	18	3	2	0
Comparison............	40	2	38	3	1	0
Multiparae						
Mentally subnormal.....	67	2	61	4	3	1
Comparison............	83	1	77	2	0	5

from an excess of forceps and breech deliveries (12 of 92) in the mentally subnormal group, compared with six of 126 in the normal comparison sample. On the other hand, within the mentally subnormal population, forceps and breech deliveries were distributed equally between CNS+ and CNS− categories and do not differ in this respect from spontaneous deliveries. In no case was the operative delivery difficult. This evidence therefore supports the conclusion that operative delivery in Aberdeen does not, of itself, seem to be of great importance in the etiology of mental subnormality.

Child. It is well known that low birth weight babies, whether the result of short gestation or of poor intrauterine growth, produce a higher than average proportion of children who are mentally retarded. In the mentally subnormal group the incidence of low birth weight babies (*i.e.*, 5½ pounds or less) is 19.6 percent (18 of 92), compared with 6.7 percent in all city children born in Aberdeen at the same time and still resident at the time of survey. Table 13 shows that, in the non-manual and craftsman group (upper social group), only one child of 19 (5 percent) weighed 5½ pounds or less at birth, compared with 17 of 73 (23 percent) in the lower social group. This difference is significant (p < 0.01). The rate of low birth weight in the upper social category in the total population was 5.7 percent, yielding a total of 203 low birth weight babies in these birth years. Only one of these 203 children was mentally subnormal. In the lower social group the rate was 7.9 percent

TABLE 13.

Distribution of birth weight by social group for mentally subnormal and comparison populations

Population and Birth Weight (pounds)	No. and Percentage of Children in Social Group					
	Upper		Lower		All	
	No.	Percent	No.	Percent	No.	Percent
Mentally subnormal						
<5½...............	1	5.3	17	23.3	18	19.6
≧5½...............	18	94.7	56	76.7	74	80.4
Total...............	19	100.0	73	100.0	92	100.0
Comparison						
<5½...............	203	5.7	255	7.9	458	6.7
≧5½...............	3370	94.3	2980	92.1	6350	93.3
Total...............	3573	100.0	3235	100.0	6808	100.0

and the number of children was 255. Of these, 17 were mentally subnormal. In other words, the lower group produces an excess of low birth weight babies and such babies run a higher risk of mental subnormality than do their counterparts in the upper social group.

The prevalence of low birth weight was higher in the CNS+ cases (Table 14). This excess is, in part, the effect of the twin pregnancies which, in turn, are related to the high incidence of severe preeclampsia. The details of each case are given in Table 15, which emphasizes again the importance of twin pregnancy and preeclampsia in the cases with evidence of central nervous system damage. Although it has long been held that low birth weight plays an important part in the etiology of mental subnormality, our data are equivocal with respect to this precise role in the causal process. However, it is by no means clear because, apart from the twin pregnancies, the low weight babies are equally divided between those with and those without evidence of central nervous system damage, and they are overwhelmingly drawn from the lower social group. One must constantly bear in mind the possibility that low birth weight may merely be symptomatic of preexisting defects in the fetus or that both the weight and the IQ are independent results of poor familial circumstances. The consideration of the intellectual level of siblings provides one way in which this possibility may be further explored.

The most striking difference between the low weight babies with and without central nervous system damage is seen in a comparison of the ability scores of the index case and its siblings. The data on IQ in Table 15 must be interpreted with caution. The mentally subnormal group were tested individually on the WISC scale, whereas the only scores available for their siblings were those on the Moray House

TABLE 14.

Relation of neurologic status to social group of low birth weight babies

Neurologic Status	No. of Children in Upper Social Group with Birth Weight (pounds)*		No. of Children in Lower Social Group with Birth Weight (pounds)*	
	<4	4–5½	<4	4–5½
CNS+..........	0	1 (1 T)	3 (1 T)	6 (2 T)
CNS−..........	0	0	1	7
Total..........	0	1 (1 T)	4 (1 T)	13 (2 T)

* T, no. of twins.

TABLE 15.

Brief case tabulation of low birth weight babies

Neurologic Status and Associated Clinical Abnormality	Gestation Period (weeks)	Pregnancy No.	Birth Weight (pounds and ounces)	Other Circumstances*	Test Score† Index case	Siblings
CNS+						
Nil	≤34	3	4–9½	1st Twin, spontaneous onset, S.D.; 2nd Twin, micrognathes	77	75
	≤34	1	3–14	1st Twin, previous myomectomy, spontaneous onset, S.D.	61	103
	≥35	1	4–5	Spontaneous onset, S.D.	67	84
	≥35	1	5–1½	Spontaneous onset, S.D.	<50	—
	≥35	4	5–7½	Spontaneous onset, S.D.	56	"Low"
Preeclampsia	≤34	2	2–15	Fibroids, aged 38, spontaneous onset, easy breech delivery	59	96
	≥35	1	5–0	2nd Twin, A.R.M., cord prolapsed, easy forceps delivery	50	126 (T)
	≥35	2	4–6	2nd Twin, A.R.M., separation of placenta, internal version, breech delivery	<50	123 (T)
Antepartum hemorrhage	≥35	4	4–9½	A.R.M., S.D.	62	107
Pyelonephritis	≤34	1	2–12	Spontaneous onset, S.D.	<50	100
CNS−						
Nil	≤34	2	4–14	Spontaneous onset, easy forceps delivery	73	81
	≤34	2	4–2¾	Spontaneous onset, S.D.	76	100
	≥35	6	4–4	Spontaneous onset, breech assisted delivery, delay with head	72	"Low"
	≥35	1	5–3	Spontaneous onset, easy spontaneous breech delivery	60	101
	≥35	7	5–0	Spontaneous onset, S.D.	69	Average, 90
	≥35	6	5–2½	Debility, A.R.M., S.D.	74	98
Antepartum	≤34	4	3–10	Spontaneous onset, S.D.	54	>80
hemorrhage	≤34	2	5–2	Spontaneous onset, S.D.	77	99

* S.D., spontaneous delivery; A.R.M., artificial rupture of membranes.
† T, twin.

Picture Intelligence Test (a group test), administered routinely to all primary school children at the age of 7. The scores, therefore, are not strictly comparable. There is also a further bias. Scores for the siblings were available only if the children were over 7 years of age and in Aberdeen schools. Therefore, the older children of large, closely spaced, and residentially stable families are overrepresented in the mean family scores. The scores of the children with central nervous system damage are exceptionally low, but in most cases the score of their siblings is either near to or considerably above average, suggesting serious damage to the index case which is not repeated. The scores of the CNS− chil-

dren are around the borderline of subnormality and the scores of none
of their siblings are in the superior range. These data suggest that, in
the CNS— group, the index case was not the only child in the family
to suffer damage, or that more general maternal, familial, and social-
cultural factors may have operated to depress the ability level of both
the mentally subnormal child and its siblings.

A General Perspective on Complication

From the above analyses it is clear that abnormality of the central
nervous system which is capable of detection by clinical examination
may occur in the absence of obstetric and perinatal complications and
that conversely serious complications may not result in clinically identifiable damage. The analytic problem is to distinguish from a mul-
tiplicity of potentially damaging factors those which are causally involved in the child's mental condition. The difficulties in making this
distinction are illustrated by the following case histories.

35/54. This case was a first pregnancy in a woman of 23 who was married
to a commercial manager. The pregnancy lasted 43 weeks and labor began
spontaneously, lasted for 32 hours, and terminated spontaneously with the
delivery of a baby weighing 5 pounds 13½ ounces. The IQ score was less than
50. The membranes were ruptured artificially 1 hour before delivery and the
liquor was heavily stained with meconium. The umbilical cord was around the
baby's neck. There was no irregularity of the fetal heart and the child cried
at once. The baby was microcephalic and had micrognathes. It is clear that
there was a primary fault in the baby which complications during the labor are
unlikely to have influenced. Fetal distress during labor, as indicated by the
passage of meconium in this case, may have been a result of the prolonged
pregnancy, but fetal distress can be caused primarily by defects in the child,
such as those present in this case. The child died at the age of 9, 1 year after
being examined in the present study.

9/54. This case was the third pregnancy of a woman aged 21. Her husband
was a laborer. She was treated in the antenatal wards for 14 days at 34 weeks
with mild preeclampsia, went home against advice, was readmitted with severe
preeclampsia, and was in labor a few days later. There was slight irregularity
of the fetal heart during the labor. The baby weighed 5 pounds 9 ounces and it
progressed well. Its IQ score was 77. The scores of siblings were 80, 67, and 66.
There was a slight rise of blood pressure with all other pregnancies but no
proteinuria. It seems clear that the preeclampsia had no identifiable effect on
the outcome.

21/53. In this case, the child was the second pregnancy of a 23-year-old
woman whose husband was a laborer. There was severe preeclampsia and a twin
pregnancy. Labor started at 38 weeks. The first child (6 pounds 3 ounces) was
delivered by forceps early and no resuscitation was required. Its IQ score at
age 7 was 123. Before the birth of the second child, partial separation of the

placenta occurred and there was some vaginal bleeding. Internal version was performed and the child was delivered as a breech without difficulty. It weighed 4 pounds 6 ounces and seemed in good condition. However, it became ill on the third day and, although intracranial hemorrhage was suspected, the child seemed to make a good recovery. The IQ score was below 50. The twins were monozygotic. A sibling born several years before had a score of 94. It seems unlikely that the preeclampsia had much to do with the damage. Relatively poor intrauterine growth of the second twin may have been a predisposing factor but the separation of the placenta and the method of delivery were probably most important.

A number of points emerge from the analysis so far. There are a host of potentially damaging circumstances and no certain method of evaluating the particular contribution of each. When the full history is considered, however, it becomes obvious that many of the obstetric factors are either incidental or of minor degree and that, even where severe complications occur, the cause of the mental subnormality may lie elsewhere. In some cases the high severity scores may be symptoms of a defect in the child unrelated to the pregnancy or they may be the result of the action, early in the pregnancy, of agents such as virus infection, a chemical substance such as thalidomide, oxygen lack, or vitamin deficiency.

Knowledge of the IQs of siblings may be useful in interpreting the findings. When the siblings of a mentally subnormal child have IQ scores within the normal range, the social, environmental, and familial explanation of the subnormality in the index child is weakened and, correspondingly, the possibility that the child has been damaged before, during, or after birth is increased. The clearest instances occur when the mentally subnormal child has an IQ under 60 and the siblings have scores well above average (*e.g.*, Case 21/53 above). An equivocal situation is produced when the mentally subnormal child has a score between 65 and 79 and when the scores of siblings fall within the same range or only slightly above it (*e.g.*, Case 9/54). In these circumstances it is necessary to take into account the obstetric histories of the siblings as well as the expected score of children in a family with these particular social characteristics.

As a first step in considering these factors, the obstetrician reviewed each mentally subnormal case to make an overall clinical judgment of the extent to which there was a departure from obstetric normality. On the assumption that such departures might increase the possibility of damage to the child, the cases were arranged in three risk categories —high, intermediate, and low. This arrangement was an attempt to get over the difficulty that a substantial score might be accumulated as the result of low scores in each of the three categories or because of a maximal score in only one. Also, a high score registered in the child might be attributable to basic defects in the child and not to the effect of a pathologic state of pregnancy or labor. For example, a child might be microcephalic or might show signs of fetal distress during labor and there might be difficulty in resuscitation. In such circumstances, even if the pregnancy were complicated by severe preeclampsia and the labor were long and difficult, it could not be claimed that the mental subnormality was the result of either of these complications. In the previous assessments of severity scores (see pages 126 and 127), the birth weight of the child by itself was not taken into account, but it has been considered in placing the case in a high, intermediate, or low risk category (see Appendix 7).

Table 16 shows the distribution of obstetric and perinatal risk categories according to neurologic status and IQ. The proportion of cases with a high or intermediate risk is clearly higher in the CNS+ group (39 percent against 21 percent). Within the CNS+ group, children with IQs of less than 50 contain a higher proportion of high or intermediate risk cases than those whose IQ is 50 or more (50 percent against 29 percent). In the CNS− group, however, there is no difference in the proportions of high and intermediate risk cases in the 50 to 59 and 60 and above IQ subgroups.

Thus, we find:

1. An association between obstetric risk and neurologic status;

2. A difference in obstetric risk within the CNS+ group according to the severity of the subnormality as measured by IQ;

3. An absence of any identifiable risk in one-third of all CNS+ children;

TABLE 16.

Relation of obstetric risk to subtype of mental subnormality

Subtype*	No. and Percentage of Children at Obstetric Risk					
	High	Inter-mediate	Low	None	Total	Percent high or intermediate
<50; CNS+	6	4	5	5	20	50⎫ 39
≧50; CNS+	5	2	7	10	24	29⎭
50–59; CNS−	0	2	1	7	10	20⎫ 21
≧60; CNS−	4	4	16	13	37	22⎭

* Defined by IQ and presence of central nervous system damage.

4. Nearly one-quarter of CNS− children with high or intermediate obstetric risk.

In Table 17 we consider the relationship of obstetric risk to both social class and subtype. In the CNS+ group as a whole, the lower class children have the higher proportion of high or intermediate risk cases (43 percent), compared with the upper class children (31 percent). Within the severely subnormal group (IQ below 50), however, the class difference is smaller, although five of the six lower class children in this group were judged to have been at high risk, compared with only one of the four upper class children. We should not, however, attach too much significance to these differences, for not only are the numbers very small, but also, severe obstetric abnormalities occur in any case more frequently in the lower social classes even in the absence of mental subnormality. This fact is further evidenced in the CNS− group, where

TABLE 17.

Relation of obstetric risk to subtype of mental subnormality and social group

Subtype*	Social Group	No. and Percentage of Children at Obstetric Risk					
		High	Inter-mediate	Low	None	Total	Percent High or Inter-mediate
<50; CNS+	Upper	1	3	2	3	9	44
	Lower	5	1	3	2	11	55
≧50; CNS+	Upper	0	1	3	3	7	14
	Lower	5	1	4	7	17	35
All; CNS+	Upper	1	4	5	6	16	31
	Lower	10	2	7	9	28	43
50-59; CNS−	Upper	0	0	0	3	3	0
	Lower	0	2	1	4	7	29
≧60; CNS−	Upper	0	0	0	1	1	0
	Lower	4	4	16	12	36	22
All; CNS−	Upper	0	0	0	4	4	0
	Lower	4	6	17	16	43	23
All	Upper	1	4	5	10	20	25
	Lower	14	8	24	25	71	31

Defined by IQ and presence of central nervous system damage.

10 of the 43 children (23 percent) were placed in the high and intermediate risk categories.

As a second step, the characteristics of the mentally subnormal children were examined in relation to the intelligence test scores of their siblings. An expected IQ score for the family was calculated based on the wife's premarital occupation, the husband's occupation at the time of the survey, and the status of the area of residence (see Chapter 7). The "expected" score is the mean score of children on the Moray House Picture Intelligence Test with a similar combination of social circumstances in the city population.

The results of these analyses for the different subtypes of mental subnormality are presented in Tables 18 to 20. In each table the data are separately arranged for upper and lower social classes. The findings for the most severely handicapped subtype (Table 18) indicate that in the upper social group only three of the nine cases had siblings whose IQs are available. Of these, one case had siblings of whom both were in the normal range—one above and one below the expected family IQ. In the second case, the sibling was at the expected level of family IQ. In the third case, two siblings were subnormal, and a third was microcephalic. There had also been three abortions—a history which suggests a possible general abnormality in the parents as reproducers.

In the lower class group, five of the children with severe mental subnormality had been judged at high obstetric risk. Four of these had siblings whose IQ scores were available. In three of these cases the IQs of siblings were around or above the expected family score. In one case the IQs of two of three siblings were low.

In Table 19, cases of the subtype of mental subnormality with IQs of 50 to 59 and signs of central nervous system damage are considered. In the upper social group, one case was classified as an intermediate risk and three were classified as low or no risk cases. Sibling scores were available for only two families; in one low risk case, the only sibling had a score of 69 but in the other, where no obstetric risk was identified, the scores of the two siblings were high.

In the lower social class the only child with a high obstetric risk weighed 2 pounds 15 ounces at birth and the IQ score of a sibling was 96. Of the others (all with no risk), one had five siblings with an average IQ score of 119, an unusually high mean score for this social group. In the other four cases the average of the sibling scores was only 85 and seven of the 21 siblings had scores of less than 75.

In Table 20, cases with IQs of 60 and above and with evidence of central nervous system damage are presented.

In Table 21, cases without evidence of central nervous system dam-

TABLE 18.

Relation of obstetric risk to family patterns of IQ in the most severely handicapped children with central nervous system damage

Social Group and Subtype*	Obstetric Risk	Obstetric Score at Stage			Ex-pected IQ†	Actual IQ	Birth Weight‡ (pounds and ounces)	IQ of Sibship§							Remarks
		Preg-nancy	Labor	Child				1	2	3	4	5	6	7	
Upper <50; CNS+	High	2	0	2	110	<50	6-5¾	<60	129						
		2	0	4	115	<50	5-12	<60							
	Interme-diate	1	2	2	≧110	<50	7-10	<60	N.S.	Ab.					
		1	2	0	110	<50	6-13	<60	N.S.	N.S.					
	Low	0	4	0	110	<50	5-13½	<60	N.S.	N.S.					
		0	1	0	112	<50	7-4	<60	<60	<60					
	None	0	0	0	106	<50	9-1	107	N.S.	N.S.					
		0	0	0	95	<50	7-6¾	N.S.	N.S.	<60					Microcephaly, died at age 9
		0	0	0	108	<50	6-2	Micro.	52	Ab.	Micro. / Ab.	<50	62	Ab.	
Lower <50; CNS+	High	2	0	4	106	<50	8-8	96	<60	N.S.					
		2	0	2	109	<50	2-12	<60	100	70	89	Ab.	N.S.	N.S.	Kernicterus Rh factor
		4	4	1	103	<50	4-6(T)	94	123	<60					Microcephaly
		4	2	1	98	<50	5-0(T)	126	<60						
	Interme-diate	0	2	2	N.S.	<50	5-15	<60							
		4	0	2	112	<50	6-3½	Ab.	<50	82	87	N.S.			Suspected mongolism
		0	4	2	110	<50	7-8	N.S.	<50	N.S.	S.B.				Suspected encephalitis at age 8 months
	Low	0	1	0	112	<50	5-11½	<60	<60	<60					
	None	0	0	0	N.S.	<50	8-10	107							
		0	0	0	110	<50	7-5¾	Ab.	Ab.	Ab.	Ab.	123	Ab.	<50	

* Defined by IQ and presence of central nervous system damage.
† N.S., not stated.
‡ T, twin.
§ IQ in italics is that of index case. Ab., abortion; Micro., microcephaly; S.B., stillbirth.

TABLE 19.

Relation of obstetric risk to family patterns of IQ in children with central nervous system damage and IQs of 50 to 59

Social Group and Subtype*	Obstetric Risk	Obstetric Score at Stage			Expected IQ	Actual IQ	Birth Weight (pounds and ounces)	IQ of Sibship†									Remarks
		Pregnancy	Labor	Child				1	2	3	4	5	6	7	8	9	
Upper 50–59; CNS+	Intermediate	4	2	0	113	50	5-14	*50*									
	Low	2	2	1	110	54	8-4	*54*									
	Low	2	0	0	110	54	9-2	69	*54*								Absence of left kidney diagnosed at age 8
	None	0	0	0	110	50	5-15	119	*50*	126	N.S.						
Lower 50–59; CNS+	High	4	1	4	105	59	2-15	96	*59*	127 (T)	117 (T)	132					
	None	0	0	0	120	55	8-2	100	122	Ab.	107	106	*55*	88	N.S.	129	
	None	0	0	0	88	59	8-0	89	104	63	67		*59*	81	N.S.	N.S., N.S. (T)	
	None	0	0	0	101	53	6-4	74	Ab.	62	N.S.	*53*	81				
	None	0	0	0	97	53	6-13	N.S.	*53*	84			64				
	None	0	0	0	95	56	5-7½	96	66		*56*	73		N.S.			

* Defined by IQ and presence of central nervous system damage.

† IQ in italics is that of index case. N.S, not stated; T, twin; Ab, abortion.

TABLE 20.

Relation of obstetric risk to family patterns of IQ in children with central nervous system damage and IQs of 60 or more

Social Group and Subtype*	Obstetric Risk	Obstetric Score at Stage			Expected IQ†	Actual IQ	Birth Weight‡ (pounds and ounces)	IQ of Sibship§								Remarks
		Pregnancy	Labor	Child				1	2	3	4	5	6	7	8	
Upper ≧70; CNS+	Low	0	0	4	96	77	4-9½ (T)	S.B.	87	*77*	75	96					Micrognathes, etc.
	None	0	0	0	120	90	5-14	99	*90*	73	62						
		0	0	0	110	70	6-13	74	70								
Lower 60-69; CNS+	High	1	0	4	97	61	3-14 (T)	*61*	103	95		Ab.	72	PPS. (24)			
		4	0	4	97	62	4-9½	107	Ab.		*62*						
		4	1	4	N.S.	64	6-4½	N.S.	N.S.	*64*	Died					Harelip and cleft palate
	Intermediate	0	4	1	112	67	4-5	67	84	N.S.	75	67	N.S.	PPS. (38)		
		0	0	1	≧90	67	8-13	N.S.	Ab.	S.S.	N.S.					
	Low	4	0	2	112	67	5-10	73	63	N.S.						
	None	0	0	0	90	62	6-6	67	42	80	*62*	Died	72	PPS. (34)	PPS. (38)	
		0	0	0	97	67	6-12	67	67		68	N.S.	PPS. (29)	59		
≧70	Low	2	1	0	75	77	5-9	80		77						
		2	0	0	98	73	8-0	Illeg.	Died	*73*	85	92	70	N.S.		
		0	0	1	106	74	7-9	98	93	74			N.S.			

* Defined by IQ and presence of central nervous system damage.
† N.S., not stated.
‡ T, twin.
§ IQ in italics is that of index case. S.B., stillbirth; Ab., abortion; PPS., postpartum sterilization (age); S.S., special school; Illeg., illegitimate.

150

TABLE 21.

Relation of obstetric risk to family patterns of IQ in children with no clinical evidence of central nervous system damage

Neurologic Status and Obstetric Risk	IQ of Index Child < 60		IQ of Index Child ≥ 60		Mean Family Score of Siblings
	Expected IQ of sibship*	IQ of sibship†	Expected IQ of sibship*	IQ of sibship‡	
			Upper Social Group		
CNS− None	120 112 <100	Ab., *51*, 104 *51* 74, Died, *55*, 102	102 — —	*72*, 102 — —	97
			Lower Social Group		
CNS− High	— — — —	— — — —	103 97 104 95	100, *76*, Died, 94, Ectopic 85, *73*, 81 98, Died, 100, 85, *74* 80, *75*, 74, N.S., Ab., N.S.	88
Interme- diate	95 — N.S.	74, 78, 83, *54*, *73*, 83 — *52*	95 104 96 112	99, 77, Ab., 89, N.S., N.S. Died, 75, 93, *67* 82, 69, 48, 66, 83, *72*, N.S. *60*, 101	85
Low	95 — — — — — — — — — — — — — —	99, 95, *59*, 96, 84, N.S. — — — — — — — — — — — — — —	98 110 95 95 85 97 104 ≧90 N.S. N.S. 104 103 112 101 N.S. 98	*86*, 77, 89, 73, 89, N.S. N.S., 89, *82*, N.S. *76*, 98, 89, 107, N.S., N.S. 104, *71*, 70, N.S. (T), N.S. (T) *75*, 71, 69, 72, N.S., N.S. S.B., 72, *80* Died, 81, *67*, 66 Died, Died, N.S., Ab., N.S., *70*, 67, N.S. *62* 109, 92; 2nd marriage, *66*, N.S., N.S. N.S., *54*, 79, 72, Died (T), *72* (T) 84, Ab., Ab., 101, *72*, 94 80, 77, 92, *78* 74, Ab., 63, *67*, 53, 81, 81 Ab., 111, 80, Ab., 81, 73, *64*, 74 Died, N.S., *70*, Ab., Ab., 79, 72, N.S., N.S., N.S.	82
None	106 — — 88 106 110 — — — — —	64, 90, 68, *55* — — 1–9 No info., N.S., *57*, 70, N.S. *59*, 67, 65, Ab., 66 70, *58*, 91, 94 — — — — —	95 99 98 89 102 91 106 75 101 105 89 89	73, *62*, Ab., 89, Ab., N.S. 91, 82, 83, 78, *60*, 62, N.S., Ab., N.S. 57, 65, 81, 65, 69, *62* S.B., *73*, 74, 97, *62*, Ab., 83 Ab., 95, 84, 89, 87, 87, *69*, 106 Died, 87, 95, 104, *87*, 80, Died, N.S., 75, 68 *67*, 59, 65, Ab., 66 80, *67*, 77, 66, N.S. N.S., 78, 67, 75, 84, *70* 86, 104, 73, 89, 73, *87*, 95 75, 65, 81, *70*, Ab., Ab., Ab., N.S. Died, Died, N.S., 85, *60*, 71, 87, 76, N.S., N.S., N.S.	77

* N.S., not stated.
† In 10 cases; IQ in italics is that of index case; No info., no information available; Ab., abortion.
‡ In 37 cases; IQ in italics is that of index case; T, twin; S.B., stillbirth.

age are shown. The upper social group contained only four of the 47 cases. Of these, three had an IQ of 50 to 59, and in two cases there were siblings with IQ scores of over 100. In the fourth case the IQ was 72 and that of the only sibling was 102. None of these cases carried any obstetric risk. The sibship evidence does suggest, however, that serious damage of undiagnosed etiology was sustained which was repeated in only one of the families.

Of the 43 cases in the lower social group, four carried a high risk and six had an intermediate risk. In only two of these 10 cases was the IQ of the index case less than 60. The expected scores were at a mean of 100, with the average IQ of the siblings in each family at 88 and 85 in the high and intermediate risk groups respectively.

In 17 cases the risk was assessed as low and in only one of these was the IQ of the index case less than 60. The average IQ of the siblings in these families was 82, as against a mean expected score of 99. There was an average of five children in a family.

In the 16 families assessed as having no obstetric risk, the average IQ of siblings was 77, as against an expected IQ of 97. Families were particularly large, and the average number of children per family was 6.6.

The salient features of the CNS— cases (Table 21) are the lower incidence of significant obstetric complications and the high incidence of large families and of siblings with IQ scores on the borderline of subnormality. The large families have occurred in spite of the availability of contraceptive advice in the city since 1946. The family size would have been still larger if postpartum sterilization had not been performed in 20 of the 47 women, in seven of them before the age of 30.

Although, in the lower social group, no definite effect of obstetric factors on the IQ of the children can be shown, the fact remains that the average IQ of the siblings falls steadily from 88 in the cases in which the obstetric risk was high to 77 when there was no obstetric risk. These findings might be taken to mean that, in those cases in which there was a substantial risk, some of the children had been damaged and thus the IQ of the siblings is considerably higher than that of the index case because presumably the damage was not repeated in other pregnancies. In the 16 cases at the bottom of the table, the very low scores are more likely to be the result of a particularly unfavorable social environment and of possibly unfavorable genetic factors. However, the possibility of generally reduced reproductive efficiency must be considered.

Conclusions

The group of mothers of the mentally subnormal children contains many more women of low socio-economic status, high parity, and poor physique than does a random cross-section of childbearing women. For this reason alone one would expect to find an excess of obstetric complications. In this analysis we have used three measures of obstetric abnormality, one based on the incidence of individual complications, one based on a scoring system which included each complication irrespective of its possible relationship to later subnormality, and a third one involving the obstetrician's judgment of the severity of the complication. With each measure we find an excess of obstetric abnormality in the pregnancy history of the mentally subnormal children.

Such findings are consistent with, but do not prove, a causal relationship between obstetric events and mental subnormality. The research problem is to identify those instances in which the relationship is merely coincidental and those in which a causal connection is either probable or certain. The difficulty is compounded by the number of instances in which two potentially damaging influences or more are present and in which, therefore, a variety of etiologic explanations are tenable. A detailed analysis of subgroups of the population, based on neurologic status, severity of intellectual impairment, and socio-economic class, is required.

In the upper social classes, defined to include the upper one-half of the general population, the prevalence of mental subnormality is relatively low but, with only a few exceptions, the children show associated clinical signs of central nervous system damage. The mothers, however, are at least as tall as women of their class in the general population and they differ only slightly with respect to parity. Further, only one baby of the 21 in this group (a twin) weighed less than 5½ pounds. Despite the high incidence of central nervous system signs, the classification of pregnancy, labor, and child into categories of obstetric risk revealed only one child with a high risk score and four with an intermediate risk score. It is clear that in these social classes the causes of very severe damage must be found elsewhere than in clinically recognizable obstetric factors in the majority of cases. Three children had microcephaly and in another there were micrognathes and other minor deformities. In one of these families, microcephaly was present in other siblings. These instances suggest the possibility of a chromosomal abnormality or an undiagnosed disturbance arising early in a particular pregnancy. Scarcity of siblings on whom an IQ measurement was available in these social classes was a serious disadvantage in sorting out the various subgroups. Two children with IQ scores of below 50, with a nil and a low obstetric risk respectively and no other obvious clinical signs, had siblings with high IQ scores, indicating severe damage to the index child which was not repeated. They are paralleled by three children with scores of above 50, without obvious obstetric factors or associated neurologic signs, in which sibling scores again are within the normal range. They provide a sharp contrast to three further children with scores of 70 or more, with associated signs of central nervous system damage, in whom obstetric risk was low or absent and in whom the scores of the index case and its siblings were not greatly dissimilar. These three families (all in Social Class IIIb) showed many of the behavioral features of the lower social classes in which an unfavorable intrauterine environment is followed by an equally unfavorable cultural and physical environment postnatally. We do not wish to give the impression that mental handicap can be ascribed precisely to a physical cause in some cases, to environmental causes in others, and to genetic causes in a further group. A single cause may be responsible in a few cases, but in most there is probably an interaction, direct or indirect, between physical and environmental "causes." In general, however, examination of the upper classes suggests a number of varying etiologic mechanisms with only occasional evidence of possible obstetric causation.

The prevalence of children with scores of below 50 and associated signs of neurologic damage is not different in the lower and the upper social classes. In many of these cases, expected scores are high and the scores of siblings, where available, are also high. More of these cases carried a high obstetric risk than did those in the upper social classes. If we were to assume that the obstetric factors were responsible for the damage, we would have to accept the conclusion that non-obstetric factors were less important in these classes than in the upper classes. There is no obvious reason why this hypothesis should be so and we are therefore constrained to accept an obstetric interpretation with some caution. The relative absence of mentally subnormal children with scores of 60 or more in the upper social classes could possibly arise because a good postnatal environment had sufficiently compensated for minimal damage to raise the child above the subnormal range; this explanation, however, can be no more than an unsubstantiated hypothesis for further research.

The lower social classes are characterized by the presence of a large group of 43 children without clinical signs of central nervous system damage. The absence of neurologic signs was paralleled by a low frequency of obstetric complications and by low sibling scores. This pattern could be the result of repeated poor reproductive performance or of general social and familial factors.

We have pointed out that alarming signs and symptoms of equal severity may appear during pregnancy and labor in two babies, one of which is subsequently found to have a high score and the other one to have a score of 50 or less. We have also drawn attention to cases where an obstetric complication occurred subsequent to a preexisting defect in the fetus. Twin pregnancy exerts a severe strain on the mother, particularly in the lower social classes, and is responsible for a quite undue proportion of the obstetric abnormalities listed in this chapter. No association has been found with duration of labor or mode of delivery. Severe preeclampsia, particularly in second and third pregnancies, was certainly more frequent than expected but its association with low birth weight and twin pregnancy makes it difficult to specify a causative effect, especially because in the twin pregnancies the second twin was unaffected. There was also a very high incidence of low birth weight. However, this condition was more frequent in the lower social classes, and in them it was often accompanied by low sibling scores. Even when taking these factors into account and considering the number of cases where chromosomal, familial, and postnatal factors could have been relevant, it seems likely that clinically recognizable obstetric factors were principally responsible for subnormality in more than one-tenth of the mentally subnormal children.

10

Retrospect and Prospect

Thus far in this report we have presented a series of detailed chapters on the design, methods, and findings of the study. We have examined the prevalence of mental subnormality and its subtypes and their associations with social, perinatal, and obstetric antecedents. In this last chapter we shall give a more overall perspective, relate the findings to views on the causation of mental subnormality, and suggest implications and further studies. We have attempted to answer certain questions about the nature and extent of ascertained subnormality in a defined population of children. Data were available on the present and antecedent characteristics of both subnormal and normal children, enabling us to determine for any particular characteristic or set of these characteristics whether there were differences between the two groups. From these findings we can draw inferences about the etiology of mental subnormality. Since obstetric complications, social factors, and genetics have all been implicated as causes of subnormality, we have paid them particular attention.

Prevalence

Between ages 8 and 10, there were 104 children who had been administratively defined as mentally subnormal and were in special schools and institutions or at home. With 8274 children at risk, the prevalence rate is 12.6 per 1000. Thirty percent of these mentally subnormal children had IQs of below 50, 20 percent had IQs of 50 to 59, and the remaining 50 percent had scores of 60 or more. The population at risk had taken a group screening intelligence test at age 7 and, of the children remaining in ordinary schools, a further 123 had scores of below 75. If these cases of psychometric subnormality are added to those administratively defined as subnormal, the prevalence becomes 27.4 per 1000.

156

In the administratively defined cases, by far the greatest proportion of mentally subnormal children came from the lower social classes, with the prevalence rate in the unskilled manual working class nine times higher than in the non-manual segments of the population. The frequent occurrence of mental subnormality in the lower social classes derived largely from the excessive representation of cases in which mental subnormality was of mild degree with IQ of 60 or higher. Within the lower social classes, mild mental subnormality was overrepresented in large families, in areas of poor housing, and where crowding was frequent. When these factors are used in combination, even more extreme elevation in prevalence was found. The rarity of cases of mild mental subnormality in the upper social class grouping is in accord with the findings of many investigations and in particular with those reported by Burt (1958) and Stein and Susser (1967) in Great Britain and by Eells et al (1951) in the United States.

Clearly, these low rates could have derived either from a true relative scarcity of such cases in the upper social groupings or as an artifact of less complete ascertainment of mild mental handicap in families better able to protect such children from the stigmatization that may attach to the label of mental subnormality. In a detailed analysis of this issue we found that the absolute number of such children in the upper classes remained very small, with the absolute number in the lower social classes four times as great. Thus, the higher rate of mild subnormality in the lower social classes was real and not an artifact of selective identification.

A fuller understanding of mental subnormality is obtained by considering the presence or absence of clinical evidence of central nervous system damage as well as the level of IQ in the children administratively defined as mentally subnormal. One-half of them had either localizing or non-localizing signs of central nervous system damage. Such damage was differentially distributed with respect to severity of intellectual impairment. With one exception all children with IQs below 50 had clear evidence of central nervous system impairment. In contrast, one-third of those with IQs of 50 or above had evidence of such damage. Three times as many of the children with IQs below 60 (the median IQ in the sample) as children with IQs of 60 or higher had such findings. In general, the more severe the intellectual deficit, the more frequent the finding of associated central nervous system damage. It is especially interesting, in view of customary tendencies to attribute mild mental subnormality to environmental and familial causes, to note that more than one-quarter of the children with IQs of 60 or higher had clinical findings of central nervous system damage. This frequency of neurologic abnormality is 10 times as high as that found in a small comparison sample of normal children. Such a finding does not support a wholly social-environmental or familial-genetic interpretation of etiology for mild mental subnormality.

There was no social class gradient for the prevalence of severe mental subnormality associated with clinical evidence of central nervous system insult. However, as might be expected from the social distribution of intelligence test scores in the mentally subnormal children, all children from families in the non-manual upper social classes had clinical evidence of central nervous system damage. Conversely, a relatively smaller proportion of the mentally subnormal children in the lowest social class had such findings. Thirty-one of the mentally subnormal children were found to be psychiatrically abnormal.

Obstetric and Perinatal Findings

Complications of pregnancy, delivery, and early infancy were present in the histories of the mentally subnormal children to a greater degree than would have been expected from their distribution in the population as a whole. Thus, moderate and severe preeclamptic toxemia, antepartum hemorrhage, breech delivery, low birth weight, short gestation, multiple births, and disturbed condition as a neonate were all overrepresented in the mentally subnormal population as a whole. One of these complications or more was present in 40 percent of the 92 children in whom such factors could be considered. As would be expected, there was a tendency for these complications to occur more frequently in the cases with associated signs of central nervous system damage. However, this difference, although suggestive, was not statistically significant because of small numbers.

Obstetric and perinatal complications frequently occur in combination rather than as single conditions of risk. Thus, as we remarked in a previous chapter, twinning usually implies low birth weight, and preeclamptic toxemia also often occurs in combination with other complications. Bearing this in mind, we noted that nine of the 11 cases in which severe or moderate preeclampsia was present showed signs of neurologic damage, as did four of the five cases of twin pregnancy. It was these two obstetric complications in particular which occurred more frequently in the subnormal group than in the population as a whole and which differentiated most clearly between the children with and without clinical evidence of neurologic damage (even when the population was matched to the subnormal group in social class and parity).

Rather than rely entirely on the presence or absence of perinatal complications, we clinically assessed the degree of risk involved in the pregnancy, birth, and condition as a neonate of each of the subnormal children. On the basis of this analysis, 15 cases were judged to have been at high risk, 12 at intermediate risk, 29 at low risk, and 35 at no risk at all. Eleven of the 15 high-risk cases had clinical findings of central nervous system damage. Of these, almost equal numbers had IQs above and below 50.

When the mentally subnormal children with high risk of obstetric scores were divided into upper and lower social class categories, 14 of the 71 cases (20 percent) fell into the lower group, whereas only 1 of the 21 cases (5 percent) fell in the upper social class category. Of the 11 cases of central nervous system damage in the high-risk infants, 10 came from the lower social group.

The Etiology of Mental Subnormality

Having summarized some of the main findings, we now move on to consider their implications for the etiology of mental subnormality. Certain general sets of causes have been advanced. These have included genetic factors, both specific and familial; complications of pregnancy, birth, and neonatal status; postnatal damage; social experience; and emotional disturbance. For a variety of reasons related to social atmosphere, background, and interest, there has been a tendency by different workers to focus relatively exclusively on one or another of these factors.

Thus, biochemists and cytogeneticists have paid primary attention to metabolic and karyosomal etiologies in severe subnormality. Workers in institutions have tended to concentrate on physiologic insult as cause and, as a function of the population of severe mentally subnormal children that they have studied, they have emphasized brain pathology as cause. Many behavioral scientists have largely been concerned with social environment and cultural disadvantage as causal agents and have worked primarily with the least severely handicapped persons. This schism of focus has been reflected most clearly in the parallel reviews of mental retardation carried out by Masland et al (1958).

A related trend has been to concentrate on particular subtypes of mental subnormality as representative of the disorder as a whole. Zigler (p. 292, 1967) has well described one expression of this tendency. He points out that "the typical textbook pictures the distribution of intelligence as normal or Gaussian in nature with approximately the lowest 3 percent of the distribution encompassing the mentally retarded.... A homogeneous class of persons is thus constructed... defined by intelligence test performance which results in a (low) score.... It is but a short step to the formulation that all persons falling below this point (70 IQ) compose a homogeneous class of 'subnormals', qualitatively different from persons having a higher IQ." The extension of statistical homogeneity to single causes has not gone unchallenged. As early as 1933, E. O. Lewis suggested that both clinical and epidemiologic evidence could be more readily assimilated if a two-group etiologic concept of mental subnormality were adopted—with one group representing individuals whose mental subnormality had derived from an anatomic or physiologic abnormality and the other reflecting a depressed level of intelligence as a result of familial inadequacies or social deprivation of experiences relevant to mental development. Since Lewis' observation, numerous workers in epidemiology, genetics, neurology, sociology, and experimental psychology, as well as others with primary concerns, have adopted one variant or another of the two-group concept (*cf.* Penrose, 1963; Hirsch, 1963; Jervis, 1959; Roberts, 1952; Burt, 1958).

It has been argued, within this general framework, that if mental handicap is severe, if clinical evidence of central nervous system damage is present, and/or if specific metabolic, chromosomal, or gene defects can be demonstrated, biologic determinance can be presumed. In the absence of such evidence, a less readily classifiable and substantiated set of influences, such as environmental deprivation, familial polygenic incompetences, or emotional disorder interfering with intellectual competence, have been suggested as causes. Our own findings emphasize the heterogeneity of the disorder and point to the need to consider different patterns of interacting causes for different subtypes of mental subnormality. From the point of view of etiology, little need be said about the children with Down's Syndrome. In a recent monograph, Penrose and Smith (1967) have considered this disorder, its distribution, its karyosomal features, and its associated psychologic attributes. They leave little doubt as to the primary relevance of chromosomal abnormalities to a clearly recognizable physical syndrome accompanied by mental deficiency. In our series, 6 percent of the cases were diagnosed with Down's Syndrome. Little, too, need be said about the one child in our series whose development was normal until he developed infectious meningoencephalitis at 2 years 10 months of age. Clear evidence of postencephalitic behavior disorder and subsequent persistent mental subnormality attest to the primary agent for mental defect. It is likely that in all of these cases functional level may have also been influenced in varying degrees by additional biologic and social factors.

For the remaining cases, attribution of cause is more complex. One step in identifying cause may be taken by considering the different subtypes of subnormality. We shall first consider those children with IQs of less than 50 who have associated clinical findings of central nervous system damage. In such cases the fact of severe intellectual impairment and the presence of brain damage make it most reasonable to attribute the mental subnormality primarily to damage to the nervous system from some cause. In our study we have sought for such cause through an examination of obstetric and neonatal events. For those cases with clinical findings of central nervous system damage but less severe degrees of intellectual impairment, the attribution of causes for mental subnormality on theoretic grounds becomes more difficult. It must be recognized that central nervous system damage can exist without attendant mental subnormality (Birch, 1964) so that in some of the cases the association among clinical findings in neurology and behavior may be adventitious rather than causal. Unfortunately, our present techniques for the clinical evaluation of neurologic status make it impossible to resolve this dilemma. In addition, these children may be particularly sensitive to adverse social, environmental, and familial circumstances. The findings are in general agreement with this interpretation.

No social class gradient was found in children with central nervous system damage and with IQ below 50. However, children with IQs above 50 and with evidence of central nervous system damage were overrepresented in the lower social classes. In these cases, then, damage to the central nervous system was more likely to have been accompanied by adverse social-environmental conditions.

The fact that the scores of the siblings of the lower class, neurologically damaged children in the moderately or mildly subnormal range tend to be low lends some weight to this argument. In the severely subnormal group, the IQ scores of the siblings vary around the mean for their social group, suggesting that the insult which resulted in the neurologic defect may, in large part, have been limited to the subnormal child. Thus, the subnormality could have resulted from the damage to the central nervous system as such, from the social-cultural milieu, from familial factors, or from their interaction.

A possible interpretation of this finding was suggested earlier. We argued that in a relatively impoverished social-cultural environment, fairly minor neurologic damage may be sufficient to depress the child's

IQ to the subnormal range. In a relatively rich environment, by contrast, such minimal damage may have less effect on the IQ, and such children, therefore, do not appear in a subnormal population.

The remaining children are those with a mild degree of intellectual impairment and with no clinical finding of central nervous system damage. This is the group to whom social and familial attributes have most frequently been assigned as etiology for the subnormality and in whom extrinsic biologic contributions have tended to be relatively ignored. In recent years, there has been some reduction in the older tendency (Goddard, 1912; Tredgold, 1952) to attribute constitutional and familial-genetic causes to this subtype of mental subnormality and there is, instead, a tendency to argue that low IQ unaccompanied by observable clinical signs of brain pathology is "subcultural" and derives from deficient environmental opportunities, from emotional disturbance, or from both (Stein & Susser, 1960; Sarason, 1959; Eells *et al,* 1951). Although one critical issue in the etiology of mental subnormality requires a separation of familial-genetic from social and environmental factors, our data do not permit valid differentiation. It is possible that no method presently available permits this distinction to be made in community surveys. What is probably required is an analysis of experiments in nature, such as appropriate monozygotic twin studies or carefully controlled large-scale intervention (Mead *et al,* 1968). At present, cytogenetic methods are not useful in considering familial and possible polygenic influences.

In our study a consideration of social class movements across generations provided no support for the suggestion that mild subnormality derives from a stagnant gene pool concentrated in the lowest social stratum and having inferior intellectual endowment or potential. Instead, we found considerable social class mobility into and out of this social stratum.

Pseudosubnormality has also been advanced as an etiologic factor. The concept suggests that it is useful to seek for a cause for mental subnormality in emotional disturbance. It suggests that such a cause is particularly frequent in milder degrees of mental impairment. We found that psychiatric abnormality was most frequently associated with severe degrees of mental subnormality and clinical evidence of central nervous system damage. This finding does not support the hypothesis of pseudosubnormality. Rather, the evidence suggests a common source for the mental subnormality and the behavior disturbance in brain damage. Such damage may directly produce disturbances or, by altering both other persons' reactions to the child and the child's own environmental responsiveness, may contribute indirectly to behavioral disorder. It is, of course, possible that a different pattern of associations will be found in other communities. For example, if a community lacks facilities for early identification and special health and educational services, it is quite possible that minimally subnormal children will be exposed to special stress and will respond by developing personality disturbances. In such instances, intellect may be additionally impaired by emotional disorder.

For the children with IQs above 50 and with no evidence of central nervous system damage, there is a clearly defined social class prevalence gradient with almost complete absence of cases in the upper social classes and considerable overrepresentation in the lowest social classes. Such findings are not unique to the present study and have been suggested for other communities as well (Burt, 1958; Stein & Susser, 1960, 1963; Goodman & Tizard, 1962; Kushlick, 1964, 1966). Further evidence suggesting that children with minimal intellectual deficit and without clinical evidence of central nervous system damage are overrepresented in families from deprived social circumstances comes from examining the family characteristics of the subnormal children with IQs of 60 and above who are most overrepresented in the lowest social classes. Our findings show that these children are overrepresented in large families living in crowded households and poor housing and where mothers have held unskilled jobs prior to marriage. Furthermore, the intelligence test scores of the siblings of these children are also lower than in comparable families without a mentally subnormal child. As we showed in Chapter 7, that section of the unskilled class which had large families and lived in substandard and overcrowded housing had a prevalence rate of this type of subnormality 8 times higher than in the population as a whole. The mean "family IQ" in this group was only 77, and more than one-half of the siblings of the mentally subnormal children either were administratively classified as subnormal or had IQs of less than 75. In absolute numbers, one-half of the children in Social Class V in this subtype had these attributes.

Having considered the etiologic implications which were drawn from a consideration of subtypes, social distributions, and family circumstances of the mentally subnormal children, we can now turn to the etiologic implications of obstetric and neonatal findings.

Obstetric and Neonatal Factors

As will be apparent from our earlier discussion, the relationship of obstetric and perinatal complications to mental subnormality is extremely complex. It must be recognized that disturbances of function do not always follow from exposure of the fetus and infant to abnormal circumstances or complications and that even when the number or severity of such complications is larger, functional capacity need not be impaired later in life. However, when complications and abnormalities of the perinatal period occur in mental subnormality, there is good reason to attempt to relate conditions of risk to the faulty mental outcome.

Investigators have, in general, pursued two paths in attempting to establish the relationship of mental subnormality to perinatal complications. On the one hand, Pasamanick and Lilienfield (1955) have argued that an excessive frequency of such complications in the histories of mentally subnormal children may be interpreted as direct evidence of increased biologic insult which potentially is capable of exerting an adverse influence on mental development. On the other hand, since pregnancy and perinatal complications tend to occur with excessive frequency in those segments of the population which, for incompletely defined social or biologic reasons, also tend to be characterized by low levels of intellectual performance, it has sometimes been argued that the relation between mental subnormality and perinatal circumstances is indirect and merely reflects an association between two sets of events which are independently present in the same population subgroupings. A particular illustration of this latter view has recently been clearly expressed by Barker (p. 21, 1966), who, when considering the frequency of unattended births in mentally subnormal children in Birmingham, has suggested that "the absence of a qualified assistant at the birth of a subnormal child (may) only reflect the low intelligence of the family into which the child is born."

In our own study, as we noted above, complications of pregnancy and the perinatal period were proportionately more common in the mentally subnormal group than in the general population, even when the population was controlled for social class. This frequency suggests that the association is not merely an artifact of the common elevation of prevalence rates for both subnormality and perinatal complications in certain social groups in the population. Again, there was a tendency for the more severe complications, especially severe preeclamptic toxemia, to be more frequently associated with the neurologically damaged than with the neurologically normal subgroups of the mentally subnormal. By contrast, those complications which are, in any case, more frequently encountered and which are associated with social class tended to occur just as often in the CNS+ as in the

CNS— groups. A case in point is low birth weight (less than 5½ pounds), which occurred with equal frequency in both subtypes.

There were, in all, 15 of the 92 subnormal children who, on detailed clinical assessment, were judged to have been at high obstetric risk. Eleven of the 15 showed evidence of central nervous system damage, and all but 1 of the 15 came from the lower social class group. Since there were 28 CNS+ children in the lower class group, there would seem to be some grounds for attributing the neurologic damage to obstetric complications in 10 (36 percent) of the 28 cases. In the upper social group, there were 16 CNS+ children only 1 of whom (6 percent) was judged to have experienced severe obstetric risk. In both social class groups the mean score of the siblings of those subnormal children in the high obstetric risk category was in the normal range and only 4 points below the score expected on the basis of their social characteristics. By contrast, the mean score of the siblings of the remaining mentally subnormal children in the CNS+ group (i.e., those not in the high obstetric risk category) was 85 against an expected score of 104.

This finding seems to give further support to the hypothesis that a proportion of cases of subnormality can be attributed to central nervous system damage, which, in turn, can be attributed to severe obstetric complications. In the present study at least, such cases are almost entirely to be found in the lower social class groups. This finding is a reflection of the greater prevalence of complications, particularly in combination, in the lower classes. Thus, severe preeclamptic toxemia combined with low birth weight and breech delivery is found almost exclusively in the lower social classes. The almost complete absence of such multiple complications in the higher social classes, where the women tended to be taller and in better physical condition, suggests that, given a good standard of care, identified obstetric complications are unlikely to be a major cause of subnormality in a healthy population. In this study, at any rate, obstetric complications might well have been the significant etiologic factor in one-quarter of the neurologically damaged group, although it is possible that an adverse postnatal environment also made a contribution in at least some cases.

In the remaining 33 cases in the CNS+ group which were not in the high obstetric risk category, there is little direct evidence as to the origin of the neurologic damage or the subnormality. In a few cases, other congenital abnormalities were present. For example, three children were microcephalic; harelip and cleft palate were present in a fourth child; there was micrognathes in a fifth; and a kidney was missing from a sixth. There were, in addition, two cases of suspected encephalitis; in another case, the baby was very ill because of severe Rh incompatibility. In a few further cases, there were other mentally subnormal children in the family, suggesting possible "familial" genetic or chromosomal influences.

We cannot, of course, claim that our estimate of obstetrically caused neurologic damage resulting in subnormality is anything other than an approximation. All that we have been able to show is that in about one-quarter of the CNS+ cases there were obstetric complications severe enough to be judged by an experienced obstetrician as likely to have caused the damage. In other cases, either there were no overt complications reported at all or, where present, the complications were judged to have been mild.

However, it must be borne in mind that the children of women in the unskilled manual classes are much less resistant to the stresses of pregnancy, labor, and the neonatal period than those in the other social classes. This weakness is shown by the very high prematurity and perinatal mortality rates from all causes and the greater tendency for these women to repeat poor reproductive performance in successive pregnancies. It is probable that children of such mothers are also more likely to sustain damage to the central nervous system. That some of the children may have sustained such damage, even in the absence of clinical signs of it, is suggested by the fact that test scores of the siblings are higher in those with a high or intermediate obstetric risk than those with a low risk or none at all.

There is further evidence of the increased vulnerability of the fetus in this social group, since it is most likely to be the result of long-standing exposure to suboptimal circumstances of the mother in the course of her growth and development. This vulnerability could operate in many ways, and the damage is unlikely to be preventable by better obstetrics *per se*. Where standards of obstetrics are high, lesions such as cerebral hemorrhage resulting from tearing of the tentorium cerebelli or severe asphyxia in the well-grown baby are relatively uncommon. Clearly, the solution lies in long-term preventive measures designed to bring the general health and development of women in all social classes up to that of the managerial and professional classes.

We are still left with the problem of severe mental subnormality in some of the children of women who are healthy and well-grown and in whom there is no high or intermediate obstetric risk. It is possible that in an early stage of pregnancy a variety of chemical and infective agents may operate on the zygote when it is particularly vulnerable.

They might not give rise to clinically recognizable signs and symptoms in the woman, however, so that diagnosis and prevention are not yet possible.

There remains the issue of obstetrics and perinatal events in the large category of mentally subnormal children in whom there was no evidence of neurologic damage. As has already been noted, in the majority of these cases, the child's IQ was above 60. Almost all were in the lower social class group, with the heaviest concentration in the unskilled manual class. This subtype of mentally subnormal children was the one in which antecedent complications were least frequently present, intellectual impairment was least severe, and clinical evidence of central nervous system damage was absent. However, low birth weight, exceptionally short mothers, and high parity were overrepresented. This evidence suggests the possibility that the mothers had defective environments as children, with resultant stunting. In general, these women were also in less good general health. Such women may well, in their pregnancy, provide an inadequate fetal environment with negative consequences for the child in the absence of definable obstetric complications. These findings emphasize the need to consider etiology in terms of factors in the mother's growth and development from the mother's own conception onward as well as the more common tendency to emphasize events from conception onward in the mentally subnormal child. The combination of poor fetal growth with subsequent suboptimal social, nutritional, and environmental opportunities may well have made a contribution to the defective development of intellect in the mother as well as in the child. Many of these children also derive from pregnancies which were fifth or later, and as a consequence they may have been affected by the mother's deteriorated status as a reproducer.

Such evidence, taken together with our previously noted finding that neurologic damage was very high in the lower class segment of the population, suggests that the view that mild mental subnormality derives from familial factors, either genetic or social-cultural, is perhaps oversimple. The conclusion warranted by our data seems to be that children born to parents who have been themselves inadequately housed, nourished, and educated are at risk to a variety of hazards—prenatal, perinatal, and postnatal—and that the combined weight of such hazards in interaction produces mental subnormality in a substantial proportion of those who survive. Improvements in the standards of medical care must be accompanied by improvement in education and social welfare if we are to reduce the numbers of minimally subnormal children.

Future Research

A number of further researches are suggested by the findings of this study. In the course of work it soon became apparent that many questions could be only tentatively pursued because of the limitations imposed by the small number of mentally subnormal children in the birth years selected for study. Further cohorts of children of the same age from other birth years in the same community must be studied if certain of these findings are to be confirmed or rejected. Moreover, new insights may be obtained by increasing the range of ages studied. Clearly, by studying older children we would anticipate an increase in the size of the least severely impaired subtype as a result of the readier identification of educational failure in children who may not be put into special educational placement until school demands are at a higher level. In such children we would expect the influences of experiential, familial, and emotional factors to be more apparent. In addition, the older the sample of children, the greater the likelihood that they will be members of completed families with siblings old enough for valid intellectual assessment. In such older groups, too, one would have the opportunity for studying children who, at earlier ages, had been put in special educational settings but who had then been returned to the regular schools.

However, the study of such older children increases the loss by out-migration and the inclusion of children by in-migrants. Such effects would increase the difficulty of relating mental subnormality to obstetric, perinatal, antenatal, and early environmental factors. Further, the higher mortality rates for severely subnormal children would be reflected in a reduction in their number relative to the less severely subnormal.

The absence of fully comparable studies in other communities makes it impossible to determine the degree to which one may generalize from our findings. The examination of similarities and differences among communities provides the only sound basis for deciding which findings are general and which are particular to given settings. For example, low birth weight appears to have adverse consequences for intellectual growth when postnatal environment is substandard but no apparent negative consequence when the environment is favorable. As a result, different associations would be expected between this variable and mental subnormality in communities that were significantly different in their social circumstances. Thus, a black child of low birth weight in an urban ghetto may be more likely to develop into a mentally subnormal child than would a white child of the same birth weight living in a high income family. Alternatively, in an egalitarian community of high living standards without poverty or especially disadvantaged subpopulations, a higher proportion of children with IQs of 60 or higher would be expected to have clinical evidence of central nervous system damage and evidence of perinatal risk than in a community with extremes of economic and social conditions. Comparative studies, therefore, provide opportunities not only for defining the general and particular associations but also for gaining further insights into the interactions among biologic, familial, and social factors in the etiology of mental subnormality.

More information is needed on the clinical neurologic status of children in regular schools who have IQs at the lower tail of the distribution for their social class. The presence of mildly subnormal children with central nervous system damage in the lower social classes and the relative absence of such children in the upper classes suggests the possibility that a minor level of damage, when combined with unfavorable postnatal developmental circumstances, results in mental subnormality, but that the same degree of damage may be insufficient to produce mental subnormality when the postnatal environment is favorable. If this is true we would expect to find an excess of central nervous system damage in upper class children in regular schools who have learning disorders, behavioral disturbances, or low intellectual competence relative to their social class.

In this study we have been able to consider a number of family characteristics and to explore their associations with mental subnormality. The findings point to links between a constellation of familial features and minimal mental subnormality. An understanding of the mechanisms underlying this association requires far more detailed information on parental intelligence and behavior, family atmosphere, life style, sibling characteristics, child-rearing practices, and family goals and values. The work of Stein and Susser (1967) on differences in intellectual outcomes in demotic and aspirant working class families, as well as our own findings, is suggestive and illustrates the potential value of such detailed study. Much more intensive work needs to be done, however, on the relationships between the child's experiences in the various milieux in which he interacts with relevant others and the development of cognitive behavior. Data from such studies, when linked to biologic inquiry, are potentially capable of improving our capacity to disentangle social-environmental, familial-genetic, and other biologic factors. In addition, they may suggest fruitful lines for effective preventive measures in families having high-risk levels for producing minimally subnormal children. Such studies, too, should include a consideration of the effects of school environment on children from such backgrounds.

To learn more about the influence of factors in the mother's early growth and development on the etiology of mental subnormality in her child, information on her social and biologic development is needed. For this purpose, the study of development across generations in stable populations is required.

At certain points in the inquiry we have been handicapped by a lack of detailed information collected in a standard form on the health and development of the child from birth to school age. It is especially necessary to have more detailed information on neonatal status and, in particular, on neonatal neurologic organization. To obtain such information requires a prospectively oriented longitudinal study of a full population or of a well-selected sample of births. In such samples, too, karyosomal and viral studies would be most valuable.

It should be noted, too, that our consideration of associations between mental subnormality and antecedent factors has been entirely retrospective and, as such, suffers from the limitations of this method (*cf.* Pasamanick & Knobloch, 1966). In essence, the retrospective method starts out with an identification of individuals who exhibit disability. It then seeks to identify patterns of antecedents which more fully typify such individuals than they do non-disabled segments of the population. Such a method in epidemiology is most useful for the identification of potential antecedent conditions of risk and for the development of hypotheses of cause. We were, of course, fortunate that our retrospective analysis could be based upon contemporaneously recorded data and so did not suffer from limitations attaching to errors of recall and missing information. This advantage was particularly important for the analysis of obstetric and perinatal antecedents. However, retrospective analysis provides no basis in a direct sense for defining the degree to which an antecedent condition or constellation of conditions is, in fact, associated with faulty outcome. Thus, although low birth weight very strongly characterized the mentally subnormal group, a retrospective analysis can give us no direct information on the degree of risk of mental subnormality that attaches to low birth weight. To answer such questions, an anterospective study starting from the condition of risk and examining the heterogeneity of outcomes is necessary. Since all of the data that we have used were contemporaneously collected it is, of course, possible to pursue such anterospectively oriented studies. These are currently in progress and will form the basis of subsequent reports.

Numerous opportunities for follow-up studies stem from the present research. It would be most interesting to be able to identify those of the subnormal children that we have studied who, after school-leaving, lose the label of mental subnormality and are absorbed into the general adult population. Which types of mentally subnormal children are eventually integrated into the work force and achieve economic independence and which do not? At present, we know that such life courses are not uncommon, but we know little about how to predict or encourage this process. Detailed follow-up of the children that we have studied would provide a basis of such knowledge.

Clearly, a common strategy underlies all of the suggestions for future work. We believe that mental subnormality is not a problem which can be effectively approached by any single scientific discipline working in isolation. The most rapid progress will occur as the result of interdisciplinary inquiries which can, in depth, analyze the interaction of biologic, social, and cultural factors affecting the growth and development of both normal and subnormal children.

References

Academy of Pediatrics, Committee on Fetus and Newborn: Nomenclature for duration of gestation, birthweight, and intra-uterine growth. *Pediatrics, 39:* 935–939, 1967.

Anastasi, A.: Intelligence and family size. *Psychol. Bull., 53:*187–209, 1956.

Anastasi, A.: *Psychological Testing.* New York: Macmillan, 1963.

Baird, D.: The cause and prevention of difficult labor. *Amer. J. Obstet. Gynec., 63:*1200–1212, 1952.

Baird, D., and Thomson, A.: The epidemiological approach in obstetrics. *Gynaecologia, 138:*226–244, 1954.

Baird, D., Thomson, A. M., and Billewicz, W. Z.: Birth weight and placental weights in pre-eclampsia. *J. Obstet. Gynaec. Brit. Emp., 64:*370–372, 1957.

Baird, D.: Environmental and obstetrical factors in prematurity, with special reference to experience in Aberdeen. *Bull. WHO, 26:*291–295, 1962.

Baird, D.: A fifth freedom. *Brit. Med. J., 2:*1141–1148, 1965.

Barker, D. J. P.: Low intelligence and obstetric complications. *Brit. J. Prev. Soc. Med., 20:*15–21, 1966.

Beier, D. C.: Behavioral disturbances in the mentally retarded. In Stevens, H. A., and Heber, R., Eds., *Mental Retardation: A Review of Research.* Chicago and London: University of Chicago Press, 1964.

Belmont, I., Birch, H. G., and Belmont, L.: The organization of intelligence test performance in educable mentally retarded subnormal children. *Amer. J. Ment. Defic., 71:*969–976, 1967.

Benda, C. E., and Farrell, M. J.: Psychopathology of mental deficiency in children. In Hoch, P. H., and Zubin, J., Eds., *Psychopathology of Childhood.* New York: Grune & Stratton, 1955.

Benton, A. L.: Psychological evaluation and differential diagnosis. In Stevens, H. A., and Heber, R., Eds., *Mental Retardation: A Review of Research.* Chicago and London: University of Chicago Press, 1964.

Bernard, R. M.: Shape and size of female pelvis. Transactions of the Edinburgh Obstetric Society, 1951–1952. *Edinburgh Med. J., 59:*1–16, 1952.

Binet, A., and Simon, T. H.: *La Mesure du Développement de l'Intelligence chez les Jeunes Enfants.* Paris: Consalant; 1911. Published in English by Williams & Wilkins, Baltimore, 1916.

Birch, H. G., Ed.: *Brain Damage in Children: The Biological and Social Aspects.* Baltimore: Williams & Wilkins, 1964.

Birch, H. G., Belmont, L., Belmont, I., and Taft, L. T.: Brain damage and intelligence in educable mentally subnormal children. *J. Nerv. Ment. Dis., 144:* 247–257, 1967.

Burt, C. L.: *The Subnormal Mind.* 2nd Edition. London: Oxford University Press, 1937.

Burt, C. L.: *The Backward Child.* 4th Edition. London: University of London Press, 1958.

Burt, C.: The inheritance of mental ability. *Amer. Psychol., 13:*1–14, 1958.

Butler, N. R., and Bonham, D. G.: *Perinatal Mortality.* Edinburgh: Livingstone, 1963.

Carter, C. H.: *Handbook of Mental Retardation Syndrome.* Springfield, Illinois: Thomas, 1966.

Clarke, A. M., and Clarke, A. D. B., Eds.: *Mental Deficiency: The Changing Outlook*. Chicago: Free Press, 1958.

Conant, J. B.: *Slums and Suburbs*. New York: McGraw-Hill, 1961.

Corner, B.: *Prematurity: The Diagnosis, Care and Disorders of the Premature Infant*. London: Cassell, 1960.

Craig, J., and Fraser, M. S.: The respiration difficulties of Caesarean babies. *Ann. Paediat. Fenn., 3*:143–152, 1957.

Cranefield, P. F.: A seventeenth century view of mental deficiency and schizophrenia: Thomas Willis on "Stupidity of Foolishness." *Bull. Hist. Med., 35*: 291–316, 1961.

Crosse, V. M.: Preliminary Results of the WHO Study on Birth Weight, a paper presented to the Expert Committee on Maternal and Child Health, World Health Organization, Geneva, 1960.

Dancis, J.: Phenylketonuria and maple sugar urine disease. *Bull. N.Y. Acad. Med., 35*:427–432, 1959.

Dawber, T. R., Kannel, W. B., and Lyell, L. P.: An approach to longitudinal studies in a community: the Framingham study. *Ann. N. Y. Acad. Sci., 107*: 539–556, 1963.

Douglas, J. W. B.: "Premature" children at primary schools. *Brit. Med. J., 1*: 1008–1013, 1960.

Douglas, J. W. B.: *The Home and the School*. London: MacGibon & Kee, 1964.

Drillien, C. M.: The social and economic factors affecting the incidence of premature birth: part I. *J. Obstet. Gynaec. Brit. Emp., 64*:161–184, 1957.

Drillien, C. M.: *The Growth and Development of the Prematurely Born Infant*. Edinburgh: Livingstone, 1964.

Eastman, N. J.: *Williams Obstetrics*. 11th Edition. New York: Appleton-Century-Crofts, 1956.

Eells, K., Davis, A., Havinghurst, R. J., Herrick, V. E., and Tyler, R. W.: *Intelligence and Cultural Differences: A Study of Cultural Learning and Problem-Solving*. Chicago: University of Chicago Press, 1951.

Ellis, N. R., Ed.: *Handbook of Mental Deficiency*. New York: McGraw-Hill, 1963.

Fairweather, D. V. I., and Illsley, R.: Obstetric and social origins of mentally handicapped children. *Brit. J. Prev. Soc. Med., 14*:149–159, 1960.

Garfield, S. L.: Abnormal behavior and mental deficiency. In Ellis, N. R., Ed., *Handbook of Mental Deficiency*. New York: McGraw-Hill, 1963.

Goddard, H. H.: *The Kallikak Family*. New York: Macmillan, 1912.

Goodman, N., and Tizard, J.: Prevalence of imbecility and idiocy among children. *Brit. Med. J., 1*:216–222, 1962.

Graham, F. K., Caldwell, B. M., Ernhart, C. B., Pennoyer, M. M., and Hartmann, A. F.: Anoxia as a significant perinatal experience: a critique. *J. Pediat., 50*:556–569, 1957.

Grimm, E.: Psychological and social factors in pregnancy, delivery and outcome. In Richardson, S. A., and Guttmacher, A. F., Eds., *Childbearing—Its Social and Psychological Aspects*. Baltimore: Williams & Wilkins, 1967.

Gruenberg, E.: Epidemiology. In Stevens, H. A., and Heber, R., Eds., *Mental Retardation: A Review of Research*. Chicago and London: University of Chicago Press, 1964.

Haggard, E. A.: Social-status and intelligence: an experimental study of certain cultural determinants of measured intelligence. *Genet. Psychol. Monogr., 49*: 141–186, 1954.

Hilliard, L. T., and Kirman, B. H.: *Mental Deficiency*. Boston: Little, Brown; London: Churchill, 1957.

Hirsch, J.: Behavior genetics and individuality understood. *Science, 142*:1436–1442, 1963.

Hunt, J. M.: *Intelligence and Experience*. New York: Ronald Press, 1961.

Illsley, R.: Environment and childbearing. *Proc. Roy. Soc. Med., 46*:53–59, 1953.
Illsley, R., Finlayson, A., and Thompson, B.: The motivation and characteristics of internal migrants. *Milbank Mem. Fund. Quart., 41*:217–248, 1963.
Illsley, R.: The sociological study of reproduction and its outcome. In Richardson, S. A., and Guttmacher, A. F., Eds., *Childbearing—Its Social and Psychological Aspects.* Baltimore: Williams & Wilkins, 1967.
James, G.: The epidemiology of mental disorder associated with damage to the brain after birth. In *Causes of Mental Disorders: A Review of Epidemiological Knowledge, 1959.* New York: Milbank Memorial Fund, 1961.
Jervis, G. A.: Studies of phenylpyruvic oligophrenia: the metabolic error. *J. Biol. Chem., 169*:651–656, 1947.
Jervis, G. A.: Juvenile amaurotic idiocy. *Amer. J. Dis. Child., 97*:663–667, 1959.
Kasius, R. V., Randall, A., IV, Tompkins, W. T., and Wiehl, D. G.: Maternal and newborn nutrition studies at Philadelphia Lying-In Hospital: newborn studies. VI. *Milbank Mem. Fund Quart., 36*:335–362, 1958.
Knobloch, H., and Pasamanick, B.: Effect of prematurity on health and growth. *Amer. J. Public Health, 49*:1164–1173, 1959.
Knobloch, H., and Pasamanick, B.: In Pasamanick, B., Ed., *Epidemiology of Mental Disorder.* Washington, D. C.: American Association for the Advancement of Science (Publication No. 60), 1959.
Knobloch, H., and Pasamanick, B.: Mental subnormality. *New Eng. J. Med., 266:* 1045–1051, 1962.
Kohn, M. L.: Social class and parent-child relationships: an interpretation. *Amer. J. Sociol., 68*:471–480, 1963.
Kushlick, A.: Subnormality in Salford. In Susser, M. W., and Kushlick, A., Eds., *A Report on the Mental Health Services of the City of Salford for the Year 1960.* Salford: Salford Health Department, 1961.
Kushlick, A.: The social distribution of mental retardation. *Develop. Med. Child Neurol., 6*:302–304, 1964.
Kushlick, A.: The prevalence of recognized mental subnormality of IQ under 50 among children in the South of England with reference to the demand for places for residential care. *Int. Copenhagen Conf. Sci. Strides Ment. Retard., 12:* 550–556, 1964.
Kushlick, A.: A community service for the mentally subnormal. *Soc. Psychiat., 1:* 73–82, 1966.
Lemkau, P. V., Tietze, C., and Cooper, M.: Mental hygiene problems in an urban district. *Ment. Hyg., 27*:279–295, 1943.
Lewis, E. E.: Report on an investigation into the incidence of mental deficiency in six areas. In *Report of the Mental Deficiency Committee, 1925–1927.* London; Her Majesty's Stationery Office, 1929.
Lewis, E. O.: Types of mental deficiency and their social significance. *J. Ment. Sci., 79*:298–304, 1933.
Lubchenko, L. O., Hansman, C., Dresser, M., and Boyd, E. S.: Intrauterine growth as estimated from live-born birth-weight data at 24–42 weeks of gestation. *Pediatrics, 32*:793–800, 1963.
MacGillivray, I.: Some observations on the incidence of pre-eclampsia. *J. Obstet. Gynaec. Brit. Emp., 65*:536–539, 1958.
MacMahon, B., and Sowa, J. M.: Physical damage to the fetus. In *Causes of Mental Disorders: A Review of Epidemiological Knowledge, 1959.* New York: Milbank Memorial Fund, 1961.
MacQueen, I. A. G.: *Aberdeen's Health and Welfare Services: An Introduction for Visitors from Overseas.* Aberdeen: Medical Officer of Health.
Maher, B.: Intelligence and brain damage. In Ellis, N. R., Ed., *Handbook of Mental Deficiency.* New York: McGraw-Hill, 1963.
Malamud, N.: Neuropathology. In Stevens, H. A., and Heber, R., Eds., *Mental*

Retardation: A Review of Research. Chicago and London: University of Chicago Press, 1964.

Martin, F. M.: Primiparae and prematurity. *Med. Officer, 91:*263–270, 1954.

Masland, R. L., Sarason, S. B., and Gladwin, T.: *Mental Subnormality: Biological, Psychological and Cultural Factors.* New York: Basic Books, 1958.

Masland, R. L.: Mental retardation. In Fishbein, M., Ed., *Birth Defects.* Philadelphia: Lippincott, 1963.

Masland, R. L.: In Pasamanick, B., Ed., *Epidemiology of Mental Disorder.* Washington, D. C.: American Association for the Advancement of Science (Publication No. 60), 1963.

McDonald, A.: Intelligence in children of very low birth weight. *Brit. J. Prev. Soc. Med., 18:*59–74, 1964.

McGehee, W., and Lewis, W. D.: The socio-economic status of the homes of mentally superior and retarded children and the occupational rank of their parents. *J. Genet. Psychol., 60:*375–380, 1942.

Mead, M., Dobzhansky, T., Tobach, E., and Light, R.: *Science and the Concept of Race.* New York: Columbia University Press, 1968.

Montague, M. F. A.: *Prenatal Influences.* Springfield, Illinois: Thomas, 1962.

Neff, W. S.: Socio-economic status and intelligence: a critical survey. *Psychol. Bull., 35:*727–757, 1938.

Neligan, G.: Gestational age, size and maturity. In Dawkins, M. J. R., and MacGregor, W. G., Eds., *Clinics in Developmental Medicine.* London: Heinemann, 1965.

Neligan, G.: The clinical effects of being "light for dates." *Proc. Roy. Soc. Med., 60:*881–883, 1967.

Nesbitt, R. E. L.: *Perinatal Loss in Modern Obstetrics.* Philadelphia: Davis, 1957.

New York State Department of Mental Hygiene: A special census of suspected referred mental retardation, Onondaga County, New York. In *Technical Report of the Mental Health Research Unit.* Syracuse: Syracuse University Press, 1955.

O'Connor, N., and Tizard, J.: *The Social Problem of Mental Deficiency.* London: Pergamon Press, 1956.

O'Connor, N.: The prevalence of mental defect. In Clarke, A. M., and Clarke, A. D. B., Eds., *Mental Deficiency: The Changing Outlook.* Chicago: Free Press, 1958.

Ogdon, D. P.: WISC IQ's for the mentally retarded. *J. Consult. Psychol., 24:*187–188, 1960.

Oldman, D., and Illsley, R.: Measuring the status of occupations. *Sociol. Rev., 14:*53–72, No. 1, 1966.

Paine, R. S., and Oppé, T. E.: *Neurological Examination of Children.* London: Spastics Society Medical Education and Information Unit, 1966.

Pasamanick, B., and Lilienfeld, A. M.: Association of maternal and fetal factors with development of mental deficiency. *J. Amer. Med. Assn., 159:*155–160, 1955.

Pasamanick, B., and Knobloch, H.: Retrospective studies on the epidemiology of reproductive casualty: old and new. *Merrill Palmer Quart. Behav. Dev., 12:*7–26, 1966.

Penrose, L. S.: *The Biology of Mental Defect.* 2nd Edition. London: Sidgwick & Jackson, 1954.

Penrose, L. S.: *The Biology of Mental Defect.* 3rd Edition. London: Sidgwick & Jackson, 1963.

Penrose, L. S., and Smith, G. F.: *Down's Anomaly.* Boston: Little, Brown, 1967.

President's Panel on Mental Retardation: *Report to the President: a Proposed Program for National Action to Combat Mental Retardation.* Washington, D. C.: U. S. Government Printing Office, 1962.

Pringle, M. L. D., Butler, N. R., and Davis, R.: *11,000 Seven Year Olds.* London: Longmans, Green, 1966.

Roberts, J. A. F.: Genetics of mental deficiency. *Eugen. Rev., 44*:71–83, 1952.

Saenger, G.: *Factors Influencing the Institutionalization of Mentally Retarded Individuals in New York City.* New York: New York State Interdepartmental Health Resources Board, 1960.

Sarason, S. B., and Gladwin, T.: In Masland, R. L., Sarason, S. B., and Gladwin, T., *Mental Subnormality: Biological, Psychological and Cultural Factors.* New York: Basic Books, 1958.

Sarason, S. B.: *Psychological Problems in Mental Deficiency.* New York: Harper, 1959.

Silverstein, A. B.: Effects of proration on the WISC IQ's of mentally retarded children. *Psychol. Rep., 12*:646, 1963.

Stein, Z., and Susser, M. W.: A study of obstetric results in an underdeveloped community: parts I and II. *J. Obstet. Gynaec. Brit. Emp., 65*:763–773, 1958.

Stein, Z., and Susser, M. W.: A study of obstetric results in an underdeveloped community: parts III and IV. *J. Obstet. Gynaec. Brit. Emp., 66*:67–74, 1958.

Stein, Z., and Susser, M. W.: The families of dull children: part 1. A classification for predicting careers. *Brit. J. Prev. Soc. Med., 14*:83–88, 1960.

Stein, Z., and Susser, M. W.: The families of dull children: part 2. Identifying family types and subcultures. *J. Ment. Sci., 106*:1296–1303, 1960.

Stein, Z., and Susser, M. W.: The families of dull children: part 3. Social selection by family types. *J. Ment. Sci., 106*:1304–1319, 1960.

Stein, Z., and Susser, M. W.: The families of dull children: part 4. Increments in intelligence. *J. Ment. Sci., 106*:1311–1319, 1960.

Stein, Z., and Susser, M. W.: The social distribution of mental retardation. *Amer. J. Ment. Defic., 67*:811–821, 1963.

Stein, Z., and Susser, M. W.: Mild Mental Subnormality: social and epidemiological studies, a paper presented to the Conference on Social Psychiatry at the 47th annual meeting of the Association for Research in Nervous and Mental Diseases, 1967.

Stevens, H. A.: Overview. In Stevens, H. A., and Heber, R., Eds., *Mental Retardation: A Review of Research.* Chicago and London: University of Chicago Press, 1964.

Stevens, H. A., and Heber, R., Eds: *Mental Retardation: A Review of Research.* Chicago and London: University of Chicago Press, 1964.

Stevenson, G. S.: In *New Directions for Mentally Retarded Children.* New York: Josiah Macy Foundation, 1956.

Stewart, D. B., and Bernard, R. M.: A clinical classification of difficult labour and some examples of its use. *J. Obstet. Gynaec. Brit. Emp., 61*:318–328, 1954.

Stoddard, G. D.: *The Meaning of Intelligence.* New York: Macmillan, 1947.

Strauss, A. A., and Lehtinen, L. E.: *Psychopathology and Education of the Brain-Injured Child.* New York: Grune & Stratton, 1950.

Susser, M. W., and Kushlick, A., Eds.: *A Report on the Mental Health Services of the City of Salford for the Year 1960.* Salford: Salford Health Department, 1961.

Thomson, A. M.: The diagnosis of malnutrition in well-nourished communities. *Amer. J. Clin. Nutr.,* 4:647–654, 1956.

Thomson, A. M.: Maternal stature and reproductive efficiency. *Proc. Nutr. Soc., 22*:55–60, 1959.

Thomson, A. M., and Billewicz, W. Z.: Nutritional status, maternal physique and reproductive efficiency. *Proc. Nutr. Soc., 22*:55–60, 1963.

Tizard, J.: *Community Services for the Mentally Handicapped.* London: Oxford University Press, 1964.

Tredgold, R. F.: *A Textbook of Mental Deficiency.* Baltimore: Williams & Wilkins, 1952.

Wechsler, D.: *The Measurement of Intelligence*. 3rd Edition. Baltimore: Williams & Wilkins, 1944.

Wechsler, D.: *The Wechsler Intelligence Scale for Children (Manual)*. New York: Psychological Corporation, 1949.

World Health Organization: The mentally subnormal child. *WHO Techn. Rep. Ser.* No. 75, 1954.

Yerushalmy, J.: The low-birthweight baby. *Hosp. Pract., 3*:62–69, 1968.

Zigler, E.: Mental retardation: current issues and approaches. In Hoffman, L. W., and Hoffman, M. L., Eds., *Review of Child Development Research*. 2nd Volume. New York: Russel Sage Foundation, 1966.

Zigler, E.: Familial mental retardation: a continuing dilemma. *Science, 155*:292–298, 1967.

Appendix 1
Population and Comparison Samples

In the course of this book we have used, for the purposes of comparison between the mentally subnormal children and the population from which they derive, three different comparison samples. The definitions of these samples and the procedures used in drawing them are set out below.

1. The population of children born in the years 1952 to 1954 resident in the city of Aberdeen in December 1962 totals 8274. This is the population at risk of mental subnormality.

2. All children being educated in the primary schools of the city in December 1962 were identified at that time during a city-wide study of reading attainment. For the most part, these children were born in the period October 1950 to September 1955 inclusive. In the spring of 1964, further testing was carried out in the school classes which contained such children. During the summer of that year (1964), a 1 in 5 random sample of these children was drawn for the purpose of carrying out home interviews with their parents. The total number of children in the random sample was 2743. The parents of 2511 children (91.5 percent) were interviewed between May 1964 and July 1965. Ninety-five of the 2743 children had left the city, 68 could not be traced, and the parents of 69 refused interview. This 1 in 5 random sample is used to make estimates of the population in particular risk groups in Chapter 7.

Sampling was carried out by including every child whose birth record number ended with the digit 2 or 6. Children not born in the city were allocated numbers beginning 5000, 5001, etc.

3. For the purpose of detailed comparisons of birth histories, siblings, etc. (see Chapters 7 and 9), a sample of 1 in 10 of the random sample (2) was chosen. Each of the families with children in the 1 in 5 sample was allocated a sample number, beginning with 0001. Individual children were identified by adding a further decimal digit; 0 where there

178

was only 1 child in the sample, 1 for second child, etc. In choosing the 1 in 10 sample of children (*i.e.*, 1 in 50 of the original population), every child who was born in the years 1952 to 1954 and whose family sample number ended in the digit 5 was included. This method of sampling yielded 148 cases. For sibling comparisons, obstetric histories, etc., those of the 148 whose parents had not been interviewed and those born outside the city were excluded. The remainder, 126 children, constitute the comparison group used for such comparisons in Chapters 7 and 9.

It should be borne in mind that, by excluding those not interviewed and those born outside Aberdeen, only the stable population is sampled—a built-in bias. In terms of the social class distribution, the bias is toward the lower social classes—the least mobile section of the population.

Appendix 2

Form to Show the Basis for Calculating the Salford Point Prevalence Rate of Mild Mental Subnormality Given in Table 1, Chapter 3, and Compared with E. O. Lewis' Rates

Number of ascertained cases 1955 to 1959 aged 7 to 10 years = 320.

Average number of children aged 7 to 10 years registered in school in each year, 1955 to 1959 = 19,500.

We assume that the number of children aged 7, 8, 9, or 10 in each year was approximately equal. Various rates of ascertainment per 1000 calculated were derived from these data.

Average Annual Incidence in Average Registered School Population.

$$(320/5) \times (1/19{,}500) \times 1000 = 3.28 \text{ per } 1000$$
$$\text{children aged 7 to 10 years.}$$

Average Point Prevalence. On the (incorrect) assumption that the chance of ascertainment is evenly distributed throughout the 4 years of ages 7 to 10 years, average duration of observation of a case = 4/2 years = 2 years. On the further assumption of a condition in equilibrium,

$$\text{Prevalence} = \text{Incidence} \times \text{Duration.}$$

Therefore, average point prevalence 1955 to 1959 in average registered school population =

$$(320/5) \times (1/19{,}500) \times (2/1) \times 100 = 6.56.$$

Point Prevalence at 10 Years of Age. On the assumption that a case once ascertained remains a case, at least up to 10 years, point prevalence at 10 years of age =

Average annual incidence accumulated through each of 4 years

of observation from ages 7 to 10 years =

$$3.28 \times 4 = 13.3.$$

This rate seems the most rigorous for comparison with Lewis. Lewis gives only prevalence data. He found point prevalence rising to a peak at 10 years, with 10 years about midpoint. Unfortunately, the point prevalence at 10 years of age cannot be calculated from his figures, and we must be content with the age-grouping 7 to 14 years.

Appendix 3
Form for Pediatric Neurologic Examination

Name of Patient_____ Age_____ Chart #_____

Examined By_____ Date of Exam._____

General
　Behavior
　　Infantile_____ Aut istic_____ Docile_____ Hyperkinetic_____

　　Normal for Age_____ Comments:_____

Speech
　Absent_____ Stutters_____ Stammers_____ Lisps_____

　Echolalia_____ Incomprehensible_____ Receptive Aphasia_____

　Expressive Aphasia_____ Comments:_____

　Cooperation During Exam: Good_____ Poor_____ General Impression of Intelligence_____

　Right/Left Handed_____ Right/Left Legged_____ Right/Left Eyed_____

　Left/Right Self Orientation: Present_____ Absent_____

　Left/Right Space Orientation: Present_____ Absent_____

　Comments:_____

　Congenital Stigmata:_____

_____

　Head Circumference:_____ Shape_____

Cranial Nerves

　I._____

　II. Gross Vision: Normal_____ Abnormal_____

　　Visual Fields by Confrontation: Normal_____ Abnormal_____

　　Fundi:_____

　III._____ IV._____ V._____ VI._____ VII._____

　VIII. Gross Hearing: Normal_____ Abnormal_____

　IX._____ X._____ XI._____ XII._____

Comments:_____

Motor: Describe:

Sitting Balance_____Standing Balance_____Crawling_____

Gait: Walking_____Running_____

Tone of Muscles: Hypotonic_____Normal_____Hypertonic_____

Comment:_____

Contractures_____Strength of Muscles_____

Coordination: Finger to Nose: Left_____Right_____

Heel to Shin: Left_____Right_____

Tandem Walking_____

Comments: (*i.e.* posturing of fingers, athetosis, etc.)_____

Reflexes   B. J.   T. J.   Abd.   Crem.   K. J.   A. J.

Left_____

Right_____

Babinsky: Yes/No_____Tonic Neck Reflexes: Left_____Right_____

Neck Righting Reflexes: Left_____Right_____

Whirling_____Moro_____Sucking_____Grasp_____Startle_____Stepping_____

Clonus: Absent_____Sustained_____Unsustained_____

Sensory:

Pin prick____Temperature_____Lt. Touch_____Position_____Vibratory_____

Double simultaneous touch perception_____

Number writing on palms_____Stereognosis_____

Comments :_____

_____

Impression:_____

_____

Prognosis: _____

Appendix 4

Form for Psychiatric Behavior Rating Scale

Name ....   Number ....

Age ....

| | Overall Psychiatric State | Normal | Abnormal | Uncertain |

if abnormal specify ....

....

....

<u>Symptoms & characteristics</u>

Mood level	No evid.	N.	Abn. High	Abn. Low	(Obs.)
	No evid.	N.	Abn. High	Abn. Low	(Rep.)

	No evid.	N.	Abn. High	Abn. Low	(Obs.)
<u>Mood consistency</u>	No evid.	N.	Abn. High	Abn. Low	(Rep.)

<u>Anxiety level</u>	No evid.	N.	Abn. High	Abn. Low	(Obs.)
(ease with which anxiety induced)	No evid.	N.	Abn. High	Abn. Low	(Rep.)

185

	No evid.	N.	Abn. High	Abn. Low	(Obs.)
Activity level (gross)	No evid.	N.	Abn. High	Abn. Low	(Rep.)
Activity level (small muscular fidgetiness, etc.)	No evid.	N.	Abn. High	Abn. Low	(Obs.)
	No evid.	N.	Abn. High	Abn. Low	(Rep.)

	No evid.	N.	Abnormal	(Obs.)
Personal relationships	No evid.	N.	Abnormal	(Rep.)

If abnormal specify ....

....

	No evid.	N.	Abn. High	Abn. Low	(Obs.)
Non-instrumental aggression (persons)	No evid.	N.	Abn. High	Abn. Low	(Rep.)
Non-instrumental aggression (objects)	No evid.	N.	Abn. High	Abn. Low	(Obs.)
	No evid.	N.	Abn. High	Abn. Low	(Rep.)

Assertiveness	No evid.	N.	Abn. High	Abn. Low	(Obs.)
	No evid.	N.	Abn. High	Abn. Low	(Rep.)

Distractibility	No evid.	N.	Abn. High	Abn. Low	(Obs.)
	No evid.	N.	Abn. High	Abn. Low	(Rep.)

Persistence	No evid.	N.	Abn. High	Abn. Low	(Obs.)
	No evid.	N.	Abn. High	Abn. Low	(Rep.)

Disorder of elimination	No evid.	Present	Absent	Uncertain	(Rep.)

If present specify ....

Disorder of eating	No evid.	Present	Absent	Uncertain	(Rep.)

If present specify ....

	No evid.	Present	Absent	Uncertain	(Rep.)
<u>Disorder of speech</u>	No evid.	Present	Absent	Uncertain	(Obs.)

If present specify ....

	No evid.	Present	Absent	Uncertain	(Obs.)
<u>Secondary habit disorder</u> (nail-biting, etc.)	No evid.	Present	Absent	Uncertain	(Rep.)

	No evid.	Present	Absent	Uncertain	(Obs.)
<u>Frank neurotic symptoms</u> (obsessional, hysterical, etc., excluding mood disturbance)	No evid.	Present	Absent	Uncertain	(Rep.)

	No evid.	Present	Absent	Uncertain	(Obs.)
"Functional" somatic symptoms (headaches, old pain, etc.)	No evid.	Present	Absent	Uncertain	(Rep.)

	No evid.	Present	Absent	Uncertain	(Rep.)
<u>Antisocial conduct</u> (theft, etc.)					

Appendix 5

Extract from Instructions to Obstetric Staff for Definition of Complications of Pregnancy (1954)

Physical Grade. An assessment of the general level of health and physique of the patient, usually made by a senior obstetrician at the time of the first antenatal examination. Originally (1948 to 1952, approximately), this assessment was made on the basis of a detailed examination of posture, muscular development, and general appearance of vitality, taking into account the condition of skin, hair, teeth, etc. Subsequently, this attempt to systematize the examination was abandoned.

$$A = \text{Very good}$$
$$B = \text{Good}$$
$$C = \text{Mediocre}$$
$$D = \text{Poor}$$
$$E = \text{Very poor}$$

Preeclampsia. *Severe.* Diastolic blood pressure rising for the first time after the 24th week of pregnancy to 90 mm. or more, recorded on at least two occasions separated by 1 day, together with proteinuria of 2 g. per liter or more not attributable to contamination or infection.

Moderate. As above, but proteinuria of 0.25 g. per liter or more, but not rising to 2 g. per liter.

"Other Hypertensive." Rise of blood pressure as above, without proteinuria, or with only a faint trace, not as much as 0.25 g. per liter. Or cases of essential hypertension, without significant proteinuria.

Placenta Previa. Antepartum hemorrhage in which placenta is definitely felt or seen to be over the cervix. Including cases without antepartum hemorrhage, *e.g.,* diagnosis made at cesarean section.

Accidental Hemorrhage. Only cases which are clinically obvious or where a retroplacental clot was found post partum.

Other Antepartum Hemorrhage. All cases not falling into the above categories, but excluding minor hemorrhage ("show") at onset of contractions.

Hemorrhage Before 29th Week. Mostly cases of threatened or inevitable abortion.

Appendix 6

Extract from Instructions to Obstetric Staff for Definition of the Physical Condition of the Neonate (1954)

Classification at Birth

In deciding the class of a baby, the condition during the *first half hour of life* should be considered.

Class A. Condition very good. The baby cries lustily within ½ minute and has good muscle tone. A baby is not in Class A if resuscitation is needed or if there is any doubt that the condition is excellent. (Extraction of loose noisy mucus does not count as resuscitation.)

Class B. Condition good but not immediately Class A. The onset of regular respiration and of crying is slightly delayed, up to 3 minutes from birth, but the condition causes no anxiety and there is steady recovery to Class A with a minimum of treatment (*e.g.,* stimulation of skin, extraction of mucus). Some babies in this class may be blue or pale or rather limp, but the heartbeat is normal.

Class C. Condition fair to poor (moderate asphyxia). Respiration is absent at first or consists of an occasional gasp. The skin is usually blue and congested, the muscle tone is normal or increased, and the heartbeat is slow and forcible. Active resuscitation is needed but the child responds to it fairly quickly; the condition becomes good within 30 minutes of birth.

Class D. Condition serious (severe asphyxia or collapse). Respiration is absent at first. The child is in a state of shock; the skin is pale and clammy, the muscles are flaccid, and the heartbeat is feeble and irregular. Active resuscitation produces only a slow response, which is incomplete within 30 minutes of birth.

Appendix 7

Details of the 10 High Obstetric Risk Cases

1. Social Class IIIb, aged 34, 5 feet 0 inches. First pregnancy, gestation 41 weeks. Health and capacity score 4. Mild preeclampsia at 36 weeks. Treated in the antenatal ward of the hospital, improved quickly. Readmitted later. Severe preeclampsia. Induction by artificial rupture of membranes (A.R.M.) but delay in starting labor. Intravenous oxytocin drip twice, eventual spontaneous delivery. No fetal distress, child weighed 6 pounds 9 ounces. Class A at birth and remained well until the third day, when a cyanotic attack developed with indrawing of the chest on breathing. Oxygen given and child improved quickly. No clinical evidence of infection although this was a possibility because of the delay in the onset of labor. Cerebral hemorrhage also suspected but there was no good reason why this condition should have occurred. Diagnosis not confirmed and baby made a good recovery and went home in the usual time. IQ score <50. Second child IQ score 129 and third, 90. (*Very suggestive of obstetric damage.*)

2. Social Class IIIc, aged 23, 5 feet 3 inches. Second pregnancy, gestation 40 weeks. Health and capacity score 4. Rh incompatibility, spontaneous delivery at term. Child very jaundiced. IQ score <50. Had an exchange transfusion. First pregnancy mild preeclampsia. Child IQ score 96. (*It seemed probable that kernicterus was the cause of the central nervous system damage. Treatment given too late.*)

3. Social Class IIIc, aged 38, 5 feet 0 inches. Second pregnancy, gestation 32 weeks. Health and capacity score 2. First pregnancy, aged 27, spontaneous delivery. Child IQ score 96. Multiple fibroids, severe preeclampsia, sterility for 8 years. Spontaneous onset of labor, easy breech delivery. Birth weight 2 pounds 15 ounces. Cyanotic attacks. IQ score 59. (*Many serious obstetric complications here and are likely to be important.*)

4. Social Class V, aged 23, 4 feet 11 inches. First pregnancy, gestation 37 weeks. Health and capacity score 4. Severe preeclampsia. After 1 week in hospital, labor induced by A.R.M. Three days' delay before labor began and contractions were poor. First twin, general anesthesia, easy forceps delivery, 6 pounds 0 ounces. Female, Class D. Very worrying symptoms for 24 hours. Had repeated cyanotic attacks and required oxygen for 24 hours. Child IQ score 126. Second twin, A.R.M., head high and a loop of cord prolapsed into vagina. Patient still under the anesthetic, forceps applied, and child delivered with ease. Weight 5 pounds, 0 ounces. Female, Class B. Made a very good recovery. No worrying symptoms at any time. IQ score <50. (*Monozygotic twins.*) Next pregnancy, child died soon after birth (polycystic kidneys). The difference in birth weight between the twins is probably of little significance. It seems strange that the first child should have such a high IQ score in view of the large amount of resuscitation which it required. (*Why was the score of the second child so low? There is no very good reason for this fact. The circumstances of the death of the next child suggest a fault in the mother.*)

5. Social Class IV, aged 16, 5 feet 7 inches. First pregnancy, gestation 29 weeks. Health and capacity score 3. Pyelitis at fifth and sixth months. Very acute attack on the second occasion, which brought on labor. Spontaneous delivery, 2 pounds 12 ounces. Many weeks in hospital. Cyanotic attacks. IQ score <50. Sibling scores 100, 89, and 72, followed by an abortion and two more children. Scores are not available for either. (*The extreme prematurity could have been an important factor here.*)

6. Social Class V, aged 19, 5 feet 3 inches. First pregnancy, gestation 40 weeks. Health and capacity score 4. Well during the pregnancy. Admitted in labor, cervix fully dilated. A.R.M. Meconium-stained liquor obtained. General anesthesia, easy assisted breech delivery. There was no fetal distress. The passage of meconium is not usually significant in the case of a breech presentation. Birth weight 5 pounds 15 ounces. Placenta weighed 15 ounces. Color was poor at birth but the child cried lustily in a very short time. There was, however, some indrawing of the chest on respiration. The placenta contained two large infarctions, which may have interfered with fetal growth. IQ score <50. Second child, 7 pounds 10 ounces. Class A. Third child, cord tightly around the neck and there was a slow response to resuscitation. Weight 5 pounds 13 ounces. Placenta weighed 1 pound 4 ounces and seemed healthy. IQ scores of the siblings not known. (*One could not be sure that the obstetric factors in the first case were responsible for the low*

IQ. It is true that the first baby weighed only 5 pounds 15 ounces and the second, 7 pounds 10¾ ounces, but the third, which was also a male, weighed 5 pounds 13½ ounces, at 40 weeks and the placenta did not contain infarctions and, indeed, seemed healthy. It is most unfortunate that sibling scores are not available.)

7. Social Class V, aged 31, 5 feet 4 inches. Second pregnancy, gestation 38 weeks. Health and capacity score 1. First child, IQ score 94. Severe preeclampsia and twin pregnancy. Spontaneous onset of labor. First twin, easy forceps delivery, 6 pounds 3 ounces. Male child, cried at once. Class A. IQ 123. Second twin partial separation of the placenta with many clots passed. Internal version and child delivered by the breech, 4 pounds 6 ounces. Male, made a good recovery but became ill on the third day with symptoms of intracranial hemorrhage. Remained ill for 7 days. IQ score <50. Child died at age 13 (11/4/66). (*It seems almost certain that the obstetric factors were directly responsible for the damage.*)

8. Social Class V, aged 32, 5 feet 5 inches. First pregnancy, gestation 32 weeks. Health and capacity score 5. Patient had a previous myomectomy operation, which may have predisposed to the premature onset of labor, especially in a twin pregnancy. First twin, spontaneous onset of labor and spontaneous delivery, 3 pounds 14½ ounces. Male, condition at birth poor and remained poor. Was given oxygen in an incubator for 1 week. Removed for a short time but replaced in incubator for another week and then progress good. IQ score 61. Showed spasticity later. Second twin, A.R.M. Spontaneous delivery, 3 pounds 12 ounces. Condition poor from the start. Repeated cyanotic attacks and improved only gradually over the next month. IQ score 103. It is difficult to see why the IQ score of the second child should be so much higher than that of the first since it took much longer to recover after birth. (*The evidence suggests strongly that the first child has been damaged during the process of pregnancy and labor. Unfortunately, there are no other siblings.*)

9. Social Class V, aged 22, 5 feet 1 inch. Fourth pregnancy, gestation 36 weeks. Health and capacity score 6. First pregnancy, IQ score 107, second, abortion, third, IQ score 95. Severe vaginal bleeding at 36 weeks, admitted to hospital as an emergency. Bleeding continued and A.R.M. performed, followed by spontaneous delivery. Child weighed 4 pounds 9 ounces. Resuscitation was difficult and oxygen was required for 24 hours. IQ score 62. Fifth pregnancy, abortion, sixth, IQ score 72. (*In this case, one might have expected very severe damage because of the low birth weight and the baby's signs and symptoms after* *birth but, in fact, the score is not very much lower than that of the subsequent child, which was mature and had no obstetric complications.)*

10. Social Class IIIc, aged 43, 5 feet 4 inches. Third pregnancy, gestation 39 weeks. Admitted as an emergency having had several eclamptic fits. Spontaneous delivery occurred soon afterward. Child weighed 6 pounds 4 ounces. Class C. There was much mucus and oxygen was required for several days (severe asphyxia). The child made slow progress thereafter. There were two previous children but IQ scores were not available. *(The severe asphyxia at birth was attributable to a combination of circumstances; the mother was unconscious during her stay in hospital, was under the influence of sedative drugs, and died 8 hours after delivery. She was a widow and had no antenatal care. There were six eclamptic fits in all.)*

The difficulty in deciding about the significance of obstetric factors is most clearly demonstrated in the three cases of twin pregnancy.

In Case *7,* the twins were identical. The larger twin cried immediately after birth and there were no subsequent complications. The second twin was much smaller (4 pounds 6 ounces, compared to 6 pounds 3 ounces, at 38 weeks) and, because of its retarded growth, was possibly more liable to damage. In addition, the placenta separated prematurely and this event led to rapid delivery by the breech. He showed evidence of intracranial hemorrhage on the third day. Finally, the IQ scores of the babies were very different. Another sibling had a score of 96. All of the evidence in this case points to obstetric damage.

In Case *8,* the situation is not quite so clear. Both babies were small but the weights were not much out of keeping with the gestation period. Both showed very alarming signs and symptoms for weeks after birth, especially the second, but the first had an IQ score of 61 and had a gross physical lesion, while the second had a score of 103, which is well up to the expected family score. In view of the grave condition of both babies after birth, it seems strange that the end results should be so different. The fact that the lowest score was 61 rather than <50 suggests that perhaps scores of this level are quite typical of the effects of severe obstetric complications.

In Case *4,* the findings are even more confusing. There was severe preeclampsia and a long interval between rupture of the membranes and the onset of labor but, unfortunately, no evidence of infection could be found which would explain the condition. Labor was long because of weak uterine contractions and the first child had very worrying signs and symptoms for 24 hours, yet the IQ score was as high as 126. The expected score was only 98. Although the cord of the second child came down when the membranes of the second sac were ruptured, delivery was completed easily and the child was very little affected, yet the IQ score was <50. She weighed 5 pounds at birth, compared to 6 pounds for the first child.

Since the gestation period was only 37 weeks, a birth weight of only 5 pounds does not represent poor intrauterine growth, especially in a twin pregnancy. The fact that the babies were of the same sex and were monozygotic increases the difficulty in explaining the great differences in IQ score. There was one subsequent child, which died 4 minutes after it was born from polycystic disease of the kidneys. It weighed 6 pounds 14 ounces. The lethal malformation in this child suggests the possibility that there was a more fundamental cause for the very low IQ score of the second twin than obstetric damage.

Author Index

Subject Index